John W. White

White's Mount Vernon Directory, and City Guide, v. 1, 1876-77

John W. White

White's Mount Vernon Directory, and City Guide, v. 1, 1876-77

ISBN/EAN: 9783337289102

Printed in Europe, USA, Canada, Australia, Japan

Cover: Foto ©Lupo / pixelio.de

More available books at **www.hansebooks.com**

WHITE'S

MOUNT VERNON

DIRECTORY,

AND

CITY GUIDE.

VOLUME 1. --- 1876 --- 1877.

TO WHICH IS ADDED

BIOGRAPHICAL SKETCHES

OF A FEW OF OUR AGED AND VENERABLE CITIZENS,

UNDER THE HEAD OF

"THREE SCORE AND TEN."

COMPILED BY

JOHN W. WHITE.

MOUNT VERNON, OHIO.

PRINTED AT THE ARGUS BOOK & JOB OFFICE, GAMBIER, OHIO.

1281155

INTRODUCTION.

A WORD or two of apology is due my patrons for the delay in the appearance of the DIRECTORY,—the first day of November last was the time the Compiler intended for its appearance. On the 14th day of June, 1875, I was stricken down with sickness—so severe, that the following December found me just able to be about, yet not strong enough for hardy exercise. In May, 1876, I commenced taking an enumeration of the City, but my last year's disease returning, enfeebled me so much that the work was not completed until about the first day of July following. Being my own type-setter, made it an arduous undertaking, without the lingering effects of my two summers' illness, which compelled me to stop work at different times for three or four days, and even for a week at a time. This is my apology for appearing before you at this late day.

To compensate my patrons for this unavoidable delay, I have given them some forty more pages than I first intended, and added such a variety of useful information, I am sure will be pleasing to my many readers. See Table of Contents.

This DIRECTORY is made up so differently from other works of the kind, that the reader will be interested in almost every page. Those seeking information as to the population of our City, by adding up the first and second columns of figures, the total result will give them the number of inhabitants—the total result of the third and fourth columns will give the number of minors under 21 years of age. According to my count, I make the population a few under five thousand. This is less than many claimed. I do not claim perfection for the DIRECTORY—but I do claim that it is an improvement on all that have been previously published. That is all I claim. Over twenty-five hundred names will be found in the DIRECTORY department alone.

The " THREE SCORE AND TEN " department will be read with deep interest. For the few sketches I have obtained, the statements made therein were given by the persons named. They will please accept my thanks. Other sketches were promised, which I should have been pleased to have procured, but my continued ill health made it impossible for me to devote the time necessary to obtained the information required.

If life and health are spared, I shall endeavor to get up another work that will contain biographical sketches of all citizens over 70 years of age, not only of this city, but will also include the whole county.

Such errors of omission or commission my kind readers may discover, I respectfully ask them to overlook, for they are more annoying to the writer than to the reader.

J. W. W.

STREET DIRECTORY.

PREPARED BY

DAVID C. LEWIS, Esq.,

CITY CIVIL ENGINEER.

1. MAIN STREET.—66 feet wide.

STREETS EAST OF MAIN, RUNNING NORTH AND SOUTH.

2. Gay street.—66 feet wide.
3. McKenzie street.
4. Park   "   Through Fair Ground near west side.
5. McArthur street.
6. Ridgely   "
7. Division street.
8. Clinton   "
9. Potwin   "
10. George   "
11. Rogers   "
12. Center Run street.
13. Boynton   "

STREETS WEST OF MAIN, RUNNING NORTH AND SOUTH.

14. Mulberry street.
15. Mechanic   "
16. Sandusky   "
17. Walnut   "
18. West   "
19. Norton   "
20. Adams   "
21. Jefferson   "
22. Harrison   "
23. Jackson street.
24. Elm   "
25. Maple Avenue.
26. Prospect street.
27. Cottage   "
28. Hurd   "
29. Chester   "
30. Railroad   "

31. HIGH STREET.

STREETS SOUTH OF HIGH, RUNNING EAST AND WEST.

32. Vine street.
33. Gambier "
34. Front   "
35. Water street.
36. Oak   "
37. Cedar Avenue.

STREETS NORTH OF HIGH, RUNNING EAST AND WEST.

38. Chestnut street.
39. Coshocton Avenue.
40. Sugar street.
41. Hamtramck street.
42. Burgess   "
43. Pleasant   "
44. Plimpton   "
45. North   "
46. Lamartin Place.
47. Curtis street.
48. Elizabeth street.
49. Wooster Avenue.
50. Wooster street.
51. Scott   "
52. Calhoon   "
53. Warden   "
54. Monroe   "
55. Madison   "
56. Washington street.
57. Franklin   "

TABLE OF CONTENTS.

MISCELLANEOUS.

THREE SCORE AND TEN SKETCHES.

LVI.
NORMAN W. PUTNAM.

Mr. NORMAN W. PUTNAM, of Gambier, Ohio, was born in Windsor county, Vermont, on the 21st day of October, 1800. Came to Gambier in 1829. Was employed as clerk in the College Store, where he remained nearly five years. Was married to Miss Maria Douglass, in February, 1833, to whom were born ten children—seven now living.

From "*Hildreth's Pioneers of Ohio*," it appears that all the Putnams, of New England, descended from John Putnam, who emigrated from Buckinghamshire, England, and settled in Salem, Massachusetts, in 1634, where General Israel Putnam was born in 1717. General Rufus Putnam was born at Sutton, Worcester county, Massachusetts, in 1733. At the same place, Sutton, and not far from the same time, the grand-father of Norman Putnam was born. In regard to the exact relationship between the different branches of the Putnam family, our inform-ant is unable to determine.

LVII—LVIII.
JAMES S. AND SOPHIA A. SAWER.

Mr. JAMES SMITH SAWER, of Gambier, was born in Leiston, county of Suffolk, England, on the 12th day of October, 1804. Came to Delaware county, Ohio, in 1833. Moved to Gambier in 1834. Went back to England in 1835. Was married to Miss Sophia Adams in 1836. Mr. Sawer returned to Gambier in 1836.

Mrs. SOPHIA A. SAWER, *nee* Adams, was born in Rushangles, county of Suffolk, England, on the 12th day of June, 1806. This venerable couple have been residents of Gambier since 1836.

MOUNT VERNON.

$\cdot-\cdot$

FOR a brief sketch of MOUNT VERNON, the compiler of this work, was in hopes of being able to have secured an abler pen than his own. In this he failed. He has been forced to become his own historian. He desires the kind wishes of his fellow-citizens for the success of an undertaking he ventured upon with many doubts and fears.

HOWE'S " Early Recollections of Ohio," and the Honorable A. BANNING NORTON'S " History of Knox County, Ohio," both excellent works, has left so little to be said about the early history of our city, that it is almost impossible to write upon the subject without re-producing that upon which they both spent so much time and labor, and I do not wish to encroach upon their " manor " more than is absolutely required.

I quote a paragraph from Howe's " Recollections," on account of its being more condensed and to the point, than Mr. Norton's. Mr. Norton's account of the early settlement of our city, runs through some sixty pages of his work, and has so many personal anecdotes mixed up in the narrative, as to render it too burdensome for a work of this brief description. Howe writes:

" The early settlers of the county were mainly from the Middle States, with some of New England origin. In 1805 MOUNT VERON was laid out, and named by the proprietors of the soil, who were JOSEPH WALKER, THOMAS B. PATTERSON and BENJAMIN BUTLER." Mount Vernon was named after the family residence of General Washington. " At this time the county was thinly settled. Two years after, the principal settlers were, as far as they are recollected, the Rileys, Darlings, Shrimplius, Butlers, Critchfields, Welkers, Dials, Logues and De Witts, on the Vernon river. In other parts of the county the Hurds, the Beams, Hunts and Dimick, Kerr, Ayres, Houck, Dalrymple, Hilliard, the Youngs, Mitchells, Bryants, Knights and Walkers. In the spring of 1807 there were only three families living on the plat of Mount Vernon, viz: Benjamin Butler, tavern keeper, from Pennsylvania, Peter Coyle, and James Craig. The early settlers of the village, were, besides those named, Joseph and James Walker, Michael Click, David and William Petti-grew, Samuel Kratzer, Gilman Bryant, and Rev. James Smith, who came in 1808, and was the first Methodist clergyman."

The *ruse* played upon the Commissioners appointed to locate the Seat of Justice for the County of Knox, has been published and narrated so often, that it has become as familiar to all "as a twice told tale," consequently I refrain from giving it place in this sketch. Mr. Norton gives three versions of the affair, as re-lated to him by old settlers. Clinton, the only rival for the prize, at that time, was far ahead of Mount Vernon, submitted with a bad grace, and for over five years, made great efforts to obtain a re-hearing. But all in vain.

The first store opened in Mount Vernon, was owned by Mr. Gilman Bryant, and was situated on the lot where now stands the store of Messrs. J. C. Swetland & Co., south west corner of Main and Gambier streets. "It was a little story and-a-half sycamore cabin, where he kept powder, shot, lead, whisky, etc., for sale to the Indians, and the few whites, in 1807."—*Norton.*

"The first brick building was erected in the spring of 1815, by Mr. Gilman Bryant."—*Howe.* During the past season, this old building has been demolished, and the Honorable HENRY B. CURTIS has erected on its site one of the most substantial and beautiful public buildings in Central Ohio.

"The first church, the Old School Presbyterian, (now down,) was built about 1817. It was of brick, forty feet square, and one story high; the first Pastor was the Rev. James Scott. The first licensed preacher in the county was the Rev. William Thrift, a Baptist, from Loudon county, Virginia, who came in 1807, and travelled from house to house."—*Howe.*

Upon the site of the church just alluded to, the Presbyterian society erected a large and substantial frame church. This last building was destroyed by fire, and a few years since the mem-bers of the church erected the present beautiful edifice. The present Pastor is the Rev. O. H. Newton.

The first boundary lines of the city I recollect of seeing, though I placed but little confidence in its reliability, was given by a Mount Vernon correspondent of the Columbus *Ohio State Journal,* and appeared under date of January 9, 1869, and reads as follows:

"Mount Vernon is bounded on the north by the Fifth Ward and John H. Roberts; on the east by Gambier Hill and the butter and egg wagons of George B. Potwin; on the south by the waters of Owl Creek, the Gas Works and Arentrue's brewery; and on the west by George Raymond's tannery, and Norton's Mill Race!"

February 26, 1845, the State Legislature passed an act entitled "An Act to Incorporate the Town of Mount Vernon, in Knox county," the first section reads as follows:

SEC. 1. *Be it Ordained by the General Assembly of the State of Ohio,* That so much of the town of Mount Vernon, in the county of Knox, as is comprised in the limits hereinafter described, that is to say, all the in-lots, streets and alleys, and other public ground bordered by the same, within the old original town plat, and its several recorded and confirmed additions, together with all fractions of lots or parcels of ground lying between the old town plat and either of said additions, especially to include such fractions or portions of ground not already laid out into town lots, as lie between the south line of Hamtramck street, and the north line of Burgess street, extended between the Hamtramck addition and Norton's addition; and so much of like ground as lies south of the north line of Chestnut street, extended east to the Coshocton road, and to include one tier of in-lots of usual size on the north side of Chestnut street, so extended as aforesaid; also embracing the following grounds—commencing at Lambton Square, at the junction of the Mansfield and Wooster roads; thence along the Mansfield road to the intersection of the north line of the cross street or road, to the new grave-yard; thence along the north line of said cross street to the grave-yard lot; thence north, and so running around said grave-yard lot and including the school house lot to the south east corner thereof; thence following the aforesaid grave yard street, to the east line of the Wooster road; thence southward along the east line of the said Wooster road and the east line of Gay street, as extended to North street; thence west to Main or Market street; thence north to the place of beginning, except such lots and streets in any of said plats or additions as have been vacated; *Provided,* That this exception shall not exclude the vacated lots and streets east of Division street, and north of Front street in the eastern addition, but the same are hereby included in the limits according to the eastern boundary of said addition, as originally laid out and recorded, be and the same is hereby created into a town corporate, to be known by the name of the town of MOUNT VERNON; *Provided,* That all ground hereafter laid out and recorded as town lots, or additions to said town, by name or otherwise, if contiguous thereto, shall, from the time of being so recorded, be included within the corporate limits of said town and constitute a part thereof.

Farther provisions of the above quoted act of incorporation, divided the town into five Wards, and allotted one Councilman to each Ward, and provided for their election; and also, for the election of one Mayor, and one Recorder for the town at large. The first officers elected under this act of incorporation, were as follows: ISAAC DAVIS, Mayor—JAMES SMITH, JR., Recorder—and the following Councilmen—First Ward, J. ELLIOTT—Second Ward, JOB EVANS—Third Ward, R. C. HURD—Fourth Ward, H. B. CURTIS—Fifth Ward, CHARLES COOPER.

Farther provisions of the act provided for the election of one town Treasurer, and one town Marshal, and one Street Commissioner. For these places I find that A. C. ELLIOTT was elected as Treasurer, C. L. BENNETT, Marshal, and J. L. YOUNG, Street Commissioner.

SEC. LIX. of the Municipal Code, passed May 3, 1852, provides "for the election of two Trustees for each Ward."

"SEC. XXI. Any town which by the special act of incorporation has been divided into Wards, shall be denominated a city of the Second Class, if the Council shall so determine."—*Ohio Law, passed 1853.*

SEC. VII., of an Act to provide for the Organization of Municipal Corporations, reads in part, as follows: "No incorporated village shall be advanced to the grade of a City of the Second Class until it shall have attained a population of five thousand." —*Passed May 7, 1869.*

FIRST WORK EVER DONE ON THE STREETS OF MOUNT VERNON.

Mr. Norton, in his "History of Knox County," pages 95-6, gives this description of the first work ever done on the streets of Mount Vernon:

"Jonathan Hunt informs us he was one of the volunteer workers on the streets, at the time the Commissioners came on, (to locate the county seat,) and that Gilman Bryant sort of bossed the work, and, being a cripple, he tended on them, and gave out the whisky and water, cheering them up as he came around, saying, 'work like men in harvest, but keep sober, boys.'— Mike Click, and John Click, his brother, drove the oxen. Mike was a bully hand with a team, and made them tear up stumps, haul logs, plow, and scrape, as necessary. Men never worked better on a road than that force then did. They chopped down trees, cut off logs, grubbed, dug down rough places, filled up gulleys, burned log heaps, and made a wonderful change in the appearance of things. It was the first work ever done on the streets of Mount Vernon."

MOUNT VERNON'S PRESENT BOUNDARY LINES.

ON the 2d day of March, 1870, our City Council passed "An Ordinance Defining and Establishing the Corporate Limits of the City of Mount Vernon, Ohio." The provisions of this Ordinance, I doubt not, will be new to most of my readers, and as a part of the current history of our beautiful City, the compiler of this work feels constrained to re-produce it here entire, for the information of our citizens. The provisions of the Ordinance reads as follows:

SEC. 1. *Be it ordained by the City Council of the City of Mount Vernon,* That the City Corporation Line of the City of Mount Vernon be, and is hereby established by the following described lines, to-wit:

Beginning at the south-west corner of the north abutment of the bridge at the south end of Main street, and running thence S. 83½°, E. 20 50-100 rods along the stone wall south of John Cooper's Steam Engine Works, to the south-east angle thereof. Thence N. 83½°, E. 5 16-100 rods to the south-east angle of John Cooper's fence, on the west side of Gay street. Thence S. 83½°, E. 12 40-100 rods to the south-west corner of the Factory addition. Thence by the courses and distances bounding the south side of said addition to the south-west corner of Curtis' and Byer's lot, being lot No. 34 in said addition. Thence N. 83½°, E. 25 80-100 rods, continuing along the south line of said addition. Thence N. 74½°, E. 32 60-100 rods along said south boundary, and by the same course to a point on the east line of Ridgely street, and near the south line of Water street. Thence N. 2°, E. 1 36-100 rods on east line of Ridgely street to a point on the south side of the Springfield, Mount Vernon and Pittsburg Railroad line. Thence S. 80°, E. 38-100 rods to a White Oak 28 inches diameter, S. 73½°, E. 21 52-100 rods S. 64°, E. 27 16-100 rods along the south side of said railroad line to the center of Allen Beach's alley. Thence N. 1¾°, E. 28-100 rods along the center of said alley to a point 12 rods south of the south side of Gambier street. Thence S. 73½°, E. 114 40-100 rods on a line parallel with the south side of Gambier street to the east line of Clinton township. Thence N. 2°, E. 94 50-100 rods on said township line to the south side of the new Gambier road. Thence N. 88°, W. 37-100 rods along the south side of said road to a point in line with the east side of Center Run street. Thence N. 2°, E. 98-100 rods along the east line of Center Run street to the center of Coshocton road. Thence N. 70°, E. 14 12-100 rods along the center of said road to John Flynn's south-east corner. Thence N. 17½°, W. 13 92-100 rods to said Flynn's north-east corner in the center of the "Harkness road." Thence N. 88°, 20' W. 166 86-100 rods along the center of said road to the south-east corner of Mrs. Plimpton's lot, known as "Round Hill." Thence N. 2°, E. 41 90-100 rods along the east side of said lot, to a point in line with the north side of Cur-

tis street. Thence on said line N. 89°, W. 43 50-100 rods to the
east side of McKenzie street. Thence N. 2°, E. 24 84-100 rods to
the south line of land owned by the heirs of Rev. James Scott,
deceased. Thence N. 31½°, E. 36 50-100 rods across said Scott's
land, 10 feet north of the stable, and along the north-east side of
an alley, across and to the west side of the Wooster road.—
Thence on the west side of said road N. 40½°, E. 13 40-100 rods to
the north-east corner of John McGibney's lot. Thence N. 49½°,
W. 12 40-100 rods along the north line of said lot, to the north-
west corner thereof. Thence N. 88½°, E. 26 50-100 rods along the
north side of land owned by John McGibney to the east side of
the Cemetery. Thence N. 2°, 10', E. 39 80-100 rods on the east
side of the Cemetery to the north-east corner thereof. Thence N.
88°, 50', W. 18 92-100 rods on the north line of said Cemetery to
the east line of the Catholic Cemetery. Thence on said east line
N. 2°, 10', E. 8 60-100 rods to the north-east corner of said Cemetery. Thence S. 76½°, W. 43 8-100 rods along the north side of
said Cemetery and Mrs. Pollock's lots, to the west side of the
Mansfield road. Thence along the west side of said road N. 14°,
W. 25 75-10.0 rods to the south side of a road on the north side of
lands owned by Widow Trimble's heirs. Thence continuing
along the south side of said road S. 76½°, W. 39.80 rods to the angle
thereof. Thence S. 68°, W. 24 rods along the south line of said
road, to a point in line with Mr. Flaharty's east line. Thence on
said east line N. 15¼°, W. 12.60 rods to said Flaharty's north-east
corner. Thence S. 72°, W. 25.84 rods along the north line of Flaharty's lot to the east end of the alley north of the tannery.—
Thence across the east end of said alley N. 22°, W. 0.76 rods to
the north side thereof. Thence S. 72°, 11.68 rods on the north
line of said alley, and to the west side of Sandusky street.—
Thence on the west side of said street N. 21°, W. 6.80 rods to the
north-east corner of John Cassil's lot. Thence on the north side
of said lot S. 68¼°, W. 60.25 rods to the west side of the Baltimore
and Ohio Railroad. Thence along the west side of said railroad
to the north line of Norton's North-Western addition. Thence
S. 68½°, W. 10 rods to the north-west corner of said addition.—
Thence S. 41½°, E. 25.50 rods along the west side of said addition
to the west side of said railroad. Thence along the west side of
said rail-road by the curves and tangents thereof 156.50 rods to a
point 4 feet west of the west end of the race bridge abutment
and 9 rods north of the north line of Chestnut street. Thence N.
88¼°, W. 60.23 rods through lands of George K. Norton, James
Rogers and others to the east line of lands owned by heirs of
John Mitchell, deceased. Thence N. 1¾°, E. 7.20 rods on said
Mitchell's east line to the north-west corner of said land. Thence
N. 89°, W. 73.62 rods along the north line of said John Mitchell's, Silas Mitchell's, John Gotshall's, Sapp and Rogers' lands to
the north-east corner of lands formerly owned by Samuel Hook-
away. Thence S. 1½°, W. 91.62 rods along the east line of said
land and through lands of Israel and Devin, to a point 8¾ rods
south of the south line of Wood street extended. Thence S. 89°,
E. 115.14 rods to the west line of lot No. 10 in Norton's Southern

addition. Thence south 2°, W. along the west side of lots 10 and 11, 6.35 rods to the south-west corner of lot No. 11, the same being on the south line of said Southern addition. Thence S. 89°, E. 8 rods on the south line of said lot No. 11, to the west side of Norton street. Thence N. 2°, E. 8 rods on the west side of said street. Thence S. 89°, E. 19 rods along the south side of lots marked "S. Gray" on city map, to the west side of the Baltimore and Ohio Railroad. Thence S. 58½°, E. 22 rods along the west side of said railroad to a point on the north side of the old race. Thence S. 64°, E. 35.48 rods along the north side of the old race, to a point from which an Elm tree about 30 inches in diameter bears S. 17½°, W. 64 links distant. Thence S. 70½°, E. 35 rods to the place of beginning.

SEC. 2. That William McClelland, the City Solicitor, be and hereby is directed to prosecute the proceedings necessary to effect the annexation contemplated in Section first of this Ordinance.

SEC. 3. That the foregoing Ordinance shall take effect and be in force from and after its passage and due publication.

Passed March 2d, 1870.

JOHN W. WHITE, *President.*

Attest, O. F. MURPHY, *Clerk.*

Things to be Remembered.

——o——

A pound avoirdupois is equal to 7,000 grains.

If a stone be dropped from the hand, it will fall through 16 feet during the first second of time.

Steel is the strongest metal, but gold is the most malleable; for a cubic inch of gold can be beaten out so as to cover the floor of a room 50 feet long and 40 feet wide.

The diamond is the hardest solid; that is to say, it can scratch everything else, but nothing else can scratch it.

A cubic inch of water weighs nearly 252 grains; and, therefore, four cubic inches weigh nearly 1,000 grains.

100 cubic inches of air weigh 31 grains.

100 cubic inches of carbonic acid weigh 47 grains.

100 cubic inches of hydrogen only weigh 2 grains.

The pressure of the atmosphere will support a column of mercury 30 inches high, and a column of water more than 30 feet high.

Sound travels through air at a velocity of about 1,100 feet in one second of time.

If a musical string vibrates 50 times in one second, it emits a deep, low note; if it vibrates 10,000 times in one second, it emits a shrill, high note.

The heat required to melt a pound of ice would heat 79 pounds of water one degree. The heat required to boil away a pound of boiling water would heat 537 pounds of water one degree.

The spark from a Leyden jar lasts only the twenty-four-thousandth part of one second.—*Prof. Balfour Stewart.*

Cleveland, Mt. Vernon & Columbus Railroad.

GENERAL OFFICES, MT. VERNON.

SHORTEST AND BEST ROUTE

TO ALL POINTS IN THE

North-East and
South-West.

Connections made at CLEVELAND for all points in the East,

AND AT

COLUMBUS for points in the West and South-West.

At AKRON for all points reached by the A. & G. W. R. R.,
and at ORRVILLE for all points on P., Ft. W. & C. R. R.

Trains Run Daily, Sunday Excepted.

☞ PARTICULAR ATTENTION PAID TO SAFE AND
SPEEDY TRANSPORTATION OF PASSENGERS
AND FREIGHT.

J. A. TILTON,
GEN'L. FREIGHT AND TICKET AGENT.

G. A. JONES,
SUPERINTENDENT.

MOUNT VERNON, OHIO, 1876.

LITERARY AND OTHER SOCIETIES.

WE quote from Norton's "History of Knox County," page
270. "The first Society of a literary character, established
at Mount Vernon, was the 'Polemic Society,' in 1815,
which was kept up until 1817, and included among its members
the more talkative and social citizens. It was converted into a
Thespian Society, and was well sustained for many years. Theatrical performances were generally gotten up every winter, for
a number of years, and were very creditable to those concerned.
The object was to spend the long winter evenings agreeably—not
to make money. Lawyers, Doctors, Merchants, and Students,
lent a hand as occasion required. Among the active and valua-
ble upon the boards, were Dr. R. P. Moore, Philo L. Norton, J.
W. Warden, Charles Sager, T. G. Plummer, Jacob Davis, Wm.
Smith, S. W. Hildreth, S. W. Farquhar, Eli Miller, Henry B.
Curtis, T. W. Rogers, Isaac Hadley, John Colerick, J. S. Banning, and Calvin Hill. The exhibitions were usually at the
Court House, or at the Golden Swan Inn. (The Golden Swan
Inn building is now known as the Swetland and Banner office
corner.—White.) The clothing, equipments and scenery, were
of very rich material. One of the old actors says—' it was most
splendidly illustrated with georgeous parahernalia in most pro-
fuse variety and transcends representation.' "

In 1816 "The Mount Vernon Library Society" was formed.
In 1821-2 the young bachelors of the town formed "The Mount
Vernon Literary Society." In 1830 "The Mount Vernon Lyce-
um" was organized, and was well sustained for many years.

About the year 1830, a regular "Amateur Dramatic Association" was organized, and continued in existence until about
1840. The representations took place in the second story of the

Huntsberry building, now known as the "Old Masonic Hall." At that time the whole of the second story was one large room, and, for Theatrical purposes, answered very well. The prominent members were, F. J. Zimmerman, Wm. Thompson, James Blake, James Smith, E. C. Vore, Benj. F. Smith, Benj. Colopy, N. N. Hill, Thomas Shaw, David Brentlinger, Elijah Stevens, Alex. Elliott, and Jacob B. Brown. One farce gave our citizens great amusement, and is often spoken of yet, viz: "Raising the Wind." Among the cast of characters, now recolleced, were— "Jeremy Diddler," F. J. Zimmerman; "Peggy, the beautiful Maid at the foot of the Hill," was well sustained by Thomas Shaw. David Brentlinger was the company's Singer and Ventriloquist. The Orchestra consisted of N. N. Hill, Benj. Colopy and Alex. Elliott. Stage Managers, B. F. Smith and F. J. Zimmerman.

In 1834, a "Mechanics' Society" was organized, which continued in operation until 1840. In 1839, a society called the "Franklin," was formed for mental improvement.

"In 1850, Zohar Blair, Noah Hill, Robert Thompson, Daniel Clark, and Samuel Davis, started 'The Mechanics' Mutual Protection Association,' which, after two years, was merged in the Brotherhood of the Union, and continued till 1854."

In December, 1849, several gentlemen of Mount Vernon set about getting up a Historical Society for Knox County, and, in 1850, a constitution was drawn up and signed by "thirty-two gentlemen, fourteen of whom," writes Mr. Norton, "have passed way from earth. Twelve years have passed by, the society long since was numbered with the things that were—and this—(the "History of Knox County,")—comes the nearest to being a report of any thing that yet has emanated from any of its members."

Mr. Norton gives the names of the members of the Historical Society, which we take pleasure in copying, viz:

Hosmer Curtis, Gilman Bryant, Joseph Muenscher, M. E. Strieby, Jesse B. Thomas, James Scott, Daniel S. Norton, M. H. Mitchell, Henry B. Curtis, R. C. Hurd, R. R. Sloan, A. Banning Norton, C. P. Buckingham, G. W. Morgan, C. Delano, Walter Smith, M. W. Stamp, N. N. Hill, George Browning, Matthew Thompson, J. C. Ramsey, J. N. Burr, Samuel Israel, W. Beam, J. W. Vance, W. H. Smith, John C. Stockton, D. Potwin, John W. White, J. H. Peacock, Samuel Mower, John W. Russell. Hosmer Curtis was chosen President; G. Bryant, Vice President;

R. C. Hurd, Treasurer; Rev. J. Muenscher, Corresponding Secretary; M. E. Strieby, Recording Secretary; R. R. Sloan, Cabinet Keeper.

In 1856, Rev. Dr. Muenscher formed a new "Mount Vernon Library Society," that continued in existence till some time in 1864.

In 1856, Dr. T. Eugene Clark, Robert Buck, J. Q. Buck, Wm. A. Bounds, Thomas Wilson, C. Springer and John W. White, associated together, and formed "The Atheneum," for Amateur Theatrical representations. They were assisted by Mrs. J. Q. Buck, Miss Irene Swan, and Miss Sallie Swetnam, of Cincinnati, and Miss Julia Irvine of New York city. The association continued for two years, and numerous performances were given the citizens.

On the evening of Monday, February 16, 1874, an association of young ladies and gentlemen of this city, gave an Amateur Dramatic entertainment, at Wolff's Hall. The pieces selected were the popular drama entitled "All that Glitters is not Gold," and the laughable farce of "The Quiet Family." The *Banner*, of February 20, speaking of the first night's performance, says: "The house was crowded to overflowing, and every thing passed off to the entire satisfaction of all concerned. . . . . . . The audience were so well pleased with the performance, that it was repeated, by general request, on the next evening."

On the evening of May 4, 1874, the same association placed upon the boards the pleasing drama of "Down by the Sea," and the roaring farce of "Raising the Wind." This entertainment was given under the auspices, and for the benefit of the "MOUNT VERNON SILVER CORNET BAND." The performance of these two pieces gave as much, if not more, satisfaction, to the audience, than the peformances of February 16, and 17, 1874.

On the evening of February 25, 1876, the same association presented to our people, at Kirk Hall, "The Honeymoon," for the benefit of the "SOLDIERS' MONUMENT." The city newspapers of the day claimed that the members of the association surpassed their previous performances. The play, by request, was repeated the next evening. The Programme of "The Honeymoon," was thought worthy, by the committee, of a place in the Corner Stone of the Monument.

As an act of justice to the ladies and gentlemen composing the "Amateur Dramatic Association," of this city, as the proceeds of ALL their entertainments, were devoted to charitable and benevolent purposes, the compiler of this brief sketch, begs leave to record, for preservation, their names, which are as follows, viz:

LADIES.

Mrs. Mame C. Stahl,
" Lu. M. Buxton,
Miss Laura Bascom,
" Belle Stevens,
" Ella Davidson,
" Letitia S. Elder,

Miss Virginia Sapp,
" Clara M. White,
" Carrie Thompson,
" Clara A. Bergin,
" Martha Irvine,
" Bessie Devin.

GENTLEMEN.

Col. William C. Cooper,
" Alexander Cassil,
Capt. Will. A. Coulter,
Mr. John W. White,
" Frank R. Moore,
" Austin A. Cassil,
" D. T. Ramsey,
" L. B. Curtis,

Mr. Clifford Buxton,
" Charles M. Hildreth,
" Charles W. Pyle,
" O. H. Tudor,
" Clarence B. Harper,
" Jack Harper,
" S. H. Reynolds,
" W. G. Clucus.

In the winter of 1876, some of the scholars of the Mount Vernon High School, formed "THE PI DELTA PSI SOCIETY," and held weekly meetings. On the evening of May 26, 1876, the Society gave a Grand Dramatic Entertainment at Kirk Hall. The entertainment was highly appreciated by a large and intelligent audience. The Programme was an excellent one. Among the performers were Charles M. Pepper, Samuel R. Gotshall, Flora Stephens, Emma Shaw, Ella Shaw, Charles W. Doty, Sue Miller, May Snook, Kate E. Swetland, Jessie White, A. Wm. Marsh, Harrie Martin, Louis Lane, Frank Harper, Clara McFarland, Jennie Chapman, Mary Sapp.

June 28, 1876, the scholars of "SAINT VINCENT DE PAUL'S PAROCHIAL SCHOOL," of this city, gave a delightful entertainment at Kirk Hall. The only drawback to the Programme was its extreme length, which must have been fatiguing to the youthful performers, ranging in age from seven years to fourteen. The names of the young performers were: Katie Henegan, Belle Henegan, John Henegan, Frank Henegan, Katie Hayes, Mary Muldowney, Mary Weber Flora Bechtol, Annie Purcell, John Taugher, Julius Rogers, Mary Payne, Mary Brent, Julia Johnson, Mary McCarthy, Walter Brent, Mary Barrett, Katie Mead, Mary Mead, Mary Kelly, Mary Dermody, Bertha Brent, Annie Barrett, Maggie Henely, Annie Henegan, Ella

Weber, Lizzie Lawler, Annie Magers, Ella Sheehan, Minnie Brent, Birdie Brent, Annie Barrett, Aggie Purcell, Katie Flanagan, Thomas Connor, Emma McKane, Henry Weber, James Kelly, William Dermody, Thomas McCale, James Murphy, Clarence Sapp, Walter Porter, Fanny Taugher, Mary Reynolds, Ella Porter, Annie Brent, Willie Sapp.

THE MYSTERY OF PERFUME.

— o —

No one has yet been able to analyze or demonstrate the assential action of perfume.   Gas can be weighed, but no scents. The smallest known creatures—the very monads of life—can be caught by a microscope lens and made to deliver up the secrets of their organization; but what is it that emanates from the pouch of the musk-deer that fills a whole space for years and years with its penetrating odor—an odor that an illimitable number of extraneous substances can carry on without diminishing either its size or weight—and what is that the warm summer air brings to us from the flowers, no man has yet been able to determine.   So fine, so subtle, so imponderable, it has eluded both our most delicate weights and measures and our strongest lenses.   If we come to the essence of each odor, we should have made an enormous stride forward, both in hygiene and in chemistry, and none would profit more than the medical profession, if it could be as conclusively demonstrated that such an odor proceeded from such an such a cause, as we already know of sulphur, sulphurate hydrogen, ammonia, and the like.

WHEN Tamberlik, the famous tenor, was once in the vicinity of Vera Cruz, he was captured by Mexican brigands, together with $40,000 which he had upon his person.   Learning who he was, they persuaded him to sing for them, and were so much pleased with his performance that they restored his money and his liberty, and also gave him $2000 for the pleasure he had conferred.

BUSINESS CHANGE.

Since page 23 of the Directory went through the press, a change has occurred in the proprietorship of the REPUBLICAN. The present proprietors are Messrs. WILKINSON & KNABENSHUE.

Population of American Cities in 1870.

——o——

Albany, N. Y.,	69,432	St. Louis, Mo.,	310,864
Baltimore, Md.,	267,354	St. Paul, Minn.,	20,140
Boston, Mass.,	250,526	Salt Lake City, Utah,	12,854
Brooklyn, N. Y.,	396,099	Toledo, Ohio,	31,584
Buffalo, "	117,714	Indianapolis, Ind.,	48,244
Charleston, S. C.,	51,210	Jersey City, N. J.,	105,059
Chicago, Ill.,	298,977	Louisville, Ky.,	100,752
Cincinnati, Ohio,	216,239	Memphis, Tenn.,	40,226
Cleveland, "	92,829	Milwaukie, Wis.,	71,440
Columbus, "	31,274	Mobile, Ala.,	32,034
Detroit, Mich,	79,977	Newark, N. J.,	105,059
Galveston, Texas,	13,818	New Haven, Ct.,	50,840
Philadelphia, Pa.,	674,022	New Orleans, La.,	191,418
Pittsburgh, "	86,076	New York, N. Y.,	942,292
Providence, R. I.,	68,905	Nashville, Tenn.,	25,865
Richmond, Va.,	51,038	Vicksburg, Miss.,	12,443
Rochester, N. Y.,	62,386	Washington, D. C.,	109,199
San Francisco, Cal.,	149,473	Wheeling, W. Va.,	19,280
" in 1876,	272,345	Zanesville, Ohio,	10,011

——•—•——

Some of the Largest Cities in the Old World.

——o——

Amsterdam, Holland,	281,805	Rome, Italy,	220,532
London, Eng.,	3,251,804	Barcelona, Spain,	180,014
Liverpool, "	493,346	Madrid, "	332,024
Paris, France,	1,851,792	Tunis, Tunis,	125,000
Berlin, Prussia,	702,437	Brussells, Belgium,	171,377
Vienna, Austria,	825,165	Naples, Italy,	418,968
Munich, Germany,	170,668	Dublin, Ireland,	245,722
St. Petersburgh, Russia,	667,963	Dresden, Germany,	156,024
Moscow, "	399,321	Rio de Janeiro, Brazil,	420,000
Pekin, China,	1,648,814	Stockholm, Sweden,	135,920
Calcutta, Asia,	616,249	Yeddo, Japan,	672,748
Bombay, "	816,592	Cairo, Egypt,	313,383
Madras, "	427,771	Mexico, Mexico,	200,000
Constantinople,	1,075,000	Siangtang, Asia,	1,000,000
Soo-chow, China,	2,000,000	Lima, Peru,	150,000
Jerusalem, Asia,	25,000	Buckarest, Roumania,	141,754

——•—•——

Population of the WORLD in 1873.

——o——

EUROPE,	- 300,530,000	AMERICA,	- 84,542,000
ASIA, -	- 798,220,000	AUSTRALIA & }	
AFRICA,	- 203,300,000	POLYNESIA, }	4,438,000

TOTAL, 1,391,030,000.

CITY GOVERNMENT.

CITY ELECTION, FIRST MONDAY IN APRIL.

MAYOR,
THOMAS P. FREDRICK, Sr.—Office, Council Chamber.
CITY MARSHAL,
CALVIN MAGERS—Office, Council Chamber.
CITY TREASURER,
THE COUNTY TREASURER—Office, Court House.
CITY SOLICITOR,
WILLIAM M. KOONS—Office, Samuel Israel's Law Office.
CITY CIVIL ENGINEER,
DAVID C. LEWIS—Office, Council Chamber.
CITY CLERK,
C. S. PYLE—Office, Probate Judge's Office.
STREET COMMISSIONER,
LYMAN W. MARSH—Office, ———
TRUSTEES OF CEMETERY,
JOSEPH M. BYERS, JOHN S. BRADDOCK, O. W. HUBBELL.

CITY COUNCIL.

COUNCIL CHAMBER, East Side of Gay Street, between High and Chestnut.

CITY COUNCIL MEETS EVERY MONDAY NIGHT.

GEORGE E. RAYMOND, *President.*
CHARLES M. HILDRETH, *Vice President.*

1st Ward—JAMES M. ANDREWS,	Term expires April, 1877.
" JOHN PONTING, - -	" " " 1878.
2d Ward—A. B. MOORE, - - -	" " " 1877.
" CHARLES M. HILDRETH,	" " " 1878.
3d Ward—JEFF. C. SAPP, -	" " " 1877.
" GEORGE W. BUNN, -	" " " 1878.
4th Ward—GEORGE E. RAYMOND, -	" " " 1877.
" CHARLES G. SMITH, -	" " " 1878.
5th Ward—JOHN MOORE. - - -	" " " 1877.
" CHRISTIAN KELLER, -	" " " 1878.

4

COUNTY OFFICERS.

——— o ———

STATE SENATOR—JOHN AULT, of Wayne County.
STATE REPRESENTATIVE—ABEL HART, Jr., of Knox.
MEMBER OF CONGRESS—E. F. POPPLETON, of Delaware.
JUDGE COURT OF COMMON PLEAS—JOHN ADAMS.
CLERK   "   "   "   —WILLARD S. HYDE.
PROSECUTING ATTORNEY—CLARK IRVINE.
SHERIFF—JOHN M. ARMSTRONG.
PROBATE JUDGE—B. A. F. GREER.
AUDITOR—ALEXANDER CASSIL.
TREASURER—W. E. DUNHAM.*
RECORDER—JOHN MYERS.
SURVEYOR—J. N. HEADINGTON.
CORONER—GEORGE SHIRA.
COMMISSIONERS—SAMUEL BEEMAN,
                JOHN C. LEVERING,
                JOHN LYAL.
INFIRMARY DIRECTORS—ANDREW CATON,
                MICHAEL HESS,

————

SCHOOL EXAMINERS—ISAAC LAFEVER, Jr.,
                FRANK R. MOORE,
                J. N. HEADINGTON.

————

* LEWIS BRITTON, after the 1st October, 1876.

———•———

TOWNSHIP OFFICERS.

——— o ———

TRUSTEES—SAMUEL DAVIS,
          JOHN BOYD,
          JOHN S. ABBOTT.
TOWNSHIP CLERK—MILTON L. MILLS.
TOWNSHIP TREASURER—REUBEN N. KINDRICK.
JUSTICES OF THE PEACE—THOMAS V. PARKS, Sr.,
                JOHN D. EWING.
CONSTABLES—EDWARD M. WRIGHT,
                WALTER L. VANCE.

CITY FIRE DEPARTMENT.

—— o ——

FIRE DISTRICTS.

First District—THE FIRST WARD.
Second " *THE SECOND WARD.*
Third " *THE THIRD WARD.*
Fourth " *THE FOURTH WARD.*
Fifth " That portion of the *FIFTH WARD* lying East of Main Street.
Sixth " That portion of the *FIFTH WARD* lying West of Main Street.

FIRE ALARMS!

—— o ——

For a Fire *East of McKenzie* or *West of Sandusky Street*, give the alarm as follows: Ring the General Alarm for half a minute, then, after a pause, give the District number, viz: ONE tap of the Bell for the *First District*—TWO taps for the *Second*—THREE taps for the *Third*, etc. Then, after a pause, ring the General Alarm as before.

For a Fire between *McKenzie and Sandusky Streets*, ring the General Alarm as above, then give the District three times, (pausing after each,) and then the General Alarm given.

ENGINE HOUSES.

Steamer, Hose, and Hook and Ladder House, East side Gay, between High and Chestnut Streets.

Second Ward Engine House, West Vine St., near B. & O. R.R.

Fifth Ward Engine House, North Main St., corner Main and Wooster.

THE FIRE DEPARTMENT.

——o——

OUR BRAVE DEFENDERS.

S. H. JACKSON,—Chief Engineer.
JOHN P. KELLY, First Assistant.
W. B. BANNING, Second   "
PRINDLE PHIFER, Third   "

SAMUEL SANDERSON,)
EMMANUEL MILLER,   } Fire Wardens.
THOMAS TRICK,   )

FIRE STEAMER—"G. B. White"

THIRD WARD.

C. W. KOONS, Engineer.
SAMUEL SANDERSON, Fireman.
WILLIAM SANDERSON, Jr., Driver.

STEAMER HOSÉ COMPANY.

THIRD WARD.

Hugh Lauderbaugh, Foreman. | John M. Blocker, Secretary.
A. McCollough, 1st Assistant. | W. J. Horner, Treasurer.
Thomas Simpson, 2d   "
Thirty-two Members.

WASHINGTON FIRE COMPANY, No. 1.

FIFTH WARD.

John Moore, Foreman. | P. Allspaugh, Secretary.
John Lawler, 1st Assistant. | Frederick Kraft, Treasurer.
George Wythe, 2d   "
Forty Members.

LAFAYETTE FIRE COMPANY, No. 2.

SECOND WARD.

Isaac Errett, Foreman. | J. M. Allison, Secretary.
William Hunt, 1st Assistant. | W. A. Silcott, Treasurer.
Jack Tousley, 2d   "
Forty Members.

RESCUE HOOK AND LADDER COMPANY, No. 1.

THIRD WARD.

R. M. Johnson, Foreman. | R. B. McCreary, Secretary.
Arthur Adams, 1st Assistant. | John S. Wirt, Treasurer.
W. W. Martin, 2d   "
Twenty-Five Members.

CITY BOARD OF EQUILIZATION, 1876.

First Ward—J. C. IRVINE.
Second "   W. F. BALDWIN.
Third "   G. W. STAHL.
Fourth "   E. V. BRENT.
Fifth "   W. B. BROWN and O. SPERRY.

BOARD OF HEALTH, 1876.

T. P. FREDRICK, (Mayor,) President.

O. M. ARNOLD,	Dr. J. N. BURR,
O. SPERRY,	Dr. T. WARD,
AARON LOVERIDGE,	W. C. COOPER,

M. M. MURPHY, Secretary.

PUBLIC BUILDINGS.

COURT HOUSE, North side High, between Gay and McKenzie Streets.
COUNTY JAIL, South side Chestnut, btw. Gay & McKenzie.
MASONIC HALL, N. E. Corner of Main and Vine streets.
OLD MASONIC HALL, Nos. 111 & 113 South Main, East side.
POST OFFICE BUILDING, North side Vine St., near Main.
APOLLO HALL, S. E. Corner Main and Chestnut Streets.
WOODWARD OPERA HOUSE, S.W. Cor. Main & Vine Sts.
KIRK OPERA HOUSE, S. W. Corner Main & Public Square.
BANNING & THOMPSON'S HALL, N.W. Cor. Main & Vine.
COUNCIL CHAMBER, East side Gay, btw. High & Chestnut.
KREMLIN BLOCK, S. E. side of Public Square.
UNION SCHOOL BUILDING, N. W. Corner Mulberry and Hamtramck Streets.

PUBLIC HOUSES.

BERGIN HOUSE, S. W. Corner Main and Front Streets.
ROWLEY HOUSE, West side Main, btw. Gambier & Front.
CURTIS HOUSE, S. E. Corner Main and Public Square.
CENTRAL HOUSE, N. W. side Public Square.
WORLEY HOUSE, North side High Street, near B & O. R. R.
HUGHES' TAVERN, Junction of Columbus & Newark Roads.

THE OHIO

Mutual Relief Association,

OF URBANA,

WAS Incorporated under the General Laws of the State of Ohio, Nov. 18, 1872, and extends its relief benefits and financial aid to widows, orphans, and others, and to all healthy persons who desire to avail themselves of its objects.

THE PLAN.

The plan upon which our Society is worked is as follows:

It has created two Divisions. Each Division has three classes, A. B. and C. Persons whose ages range from 20 to 35, are assigned to Class A. Those whose ages range from 35 to 50 are placed in Class B, and those between the ages of 50 and 65 in Class C. No person is admitted into the Society whose health is permanently impaired. Terms of membership in Division No. 1, are:

Entrance or Membership Fee, - -	$3 00
Annual Dues, - - - - - -	2 00
Assessment for first two deaths in advance,	2 00
Amount to be paid down, - - -	$7 00

Which will entitle the member to a Certificate for $1,000. No more money is required of a member until a year has passed away, unless a death occurs in his or her class, in which event an assessment of $1,25, to be paid within 30 days after notice. No membership fee to be paid again. The annual dues once a year.

Certificate for $5,000, in Division No. 2, cost $25,00. Assessments, as deaths may occur in his or her class, of $5,50. Annual dues to be paid once each year, of $10,00. At death, each member's family will receive back the amount paid on death assessments, together with the contributions of his or her class.

This Company is composed out of the many wealthy, philanthrophic and public spirited citizens of Urbana, Ohio. As to their character, read the following:

AUDITOR OF STATE'S ENDORSEMENT.

"It affords me pleasure to say, from my own personal knowledge of most of the members of the Ohio Mutual Relief Association, of Urbana, Ohio, and from good information in regard to the remainder, they are gentlemen of high character, and ample responsibility. JAMES WILLIAMS, *Auditor State.*"

For further Information call on

WM. BEAM, AGENT,

Corner of Mulberry and Chestnut Streets,

MOUNT VERNON, OHIO.

NEWSPAPERS.

MT. VERNON DEMOCRATIC BANNER—[Weekly.]
Office—HOOKER BLOCK—S. W. Corner Main and
Gambier Streets. L. HARPER, Editor
and Proprietor.
WM. M. HARPER, Local Editor.

MT. VERNON REPUBLICAN—[Weekly.] Office—
KREMLIN BUILDING, S. E. Corner High street
and Public Square. J. H. HAMILTON,
Editor and Proprietor.
E. C. HAMILTON, Local Editor.

FLORAL GAZETTE—[Monthly.]—Office—No. 1, Kremlin
Block, (Up Stairs,) Corner High Street and Public Square.
GEO. PARK, Editor and Proprietor.

THE ORPHANS' FRIEND—[Monthly.]—Published at the
Floral Gazette office. Rev. G. W. McWHERTER, Editor.

COURTS—KNOX COUNTY—1876.

DISTRICT JUDGES:

WILLIAM REED, of Holmes County.
CHARLES FOLLETT, of Licking "
D. DIRLAM, of Richland "
JOHN ADAMS, of Knox "
T. J. KINNY, of Ashland "

DISTRICT COURT:

Knox County—July 5th.

Clerk—W. S. HYDE.

COURTS COMMON PLEAS:

Knox County—February 21—May 8—November 20.

Clerk—W. S. HYDE.

SIXTH JUDICIAL DISTRICT:

Composed of the following Counties:

DISTRICT AND COURTS COMMON PLEAS.

Ashland County,	Richland County,
Coshocton "	Knox "
Delaware "	Morrow "
Holmes "	Wayne "
Licking "	

SUNBURY SPECTATOR.

THE LEADING FAMILY NEWSPAPER.

SUNBURY is situated on the Cleveland, Mount Vernon and Columbus Railroad,—centrally located, and with a rapidly growing population.

The SPECTATOR is the only paper published in the town, and is a general household favorite. The career of this paper during the few years of its history, marks the success which seldom fails, when industry, perseverance, able and faithful management are united in conducting a newspaper. The SPECTATOR is a seven column folio, published every Thursday, and is in all respects a first class Journal. Nothing is admitted into its Editorial or News columns, that can offend the most fastidious sentiments or taste. Thus it is essentially a FAMILY NEWSPAPER. Its Market Reports are carefully prepared and corrected weekly. "*Independent* in all things but *Neutral* in nothing." Its opinions upon public topics are as freely and explicitly declared as they are carefully considered and adopted. Thus its influence upon public affairs is deep and strong. There are few country Journals which can present such a record, and it is one that will be accorded by all its patrons without hesitation. Its local columns are equalled by few; besides giving all the available news in its own quarters, it also has Correspondents in all the larger places around it. Its Editorials are all on the latest subjects, exposing all rascality, either at home or abroad, and are given with the best of its ability, no matter whom it praises, flatters or injures.

It weekly contains all Congressional News, besides News from the West, the East, the South, the North, from Washington, and from Foreign Lands, and one copy contains as much reading matter as any two papers published in the county. In all its items it publishes only what is truthful and reliable, making it the paper that the parent may, without fear, place before his family.

As an Advertising Medium,

The SPECTATOR cannot be excelled in the district wherein it circulates.

☞ Sample copies will be sent upon receipt of request. ☜

TERMS—$1.50 Per Year.

Address all Communications to

J. S. WATSON, Publisher,

Sunbury, Delaware County, Ohio.

TABLE OF DISTANCES.

FROM MOUNT VERNON TO	Miles.	FROM MOUNT VERNON TO	Miles.
Albany, New York,	581	Memphis, Tennessee,	652
Boston, Massachusetts,	780	Milwaukee, Wisconsin,	444
Buffalo, New York,	283	Montgomery, Alabama,	765
Baltimore, Maryland,	505	Mobile, "	943
Charleston,South Carolina,	1000	Nashville, Tennessee,'	460
Chicago, Illinois,	359	New Orleans, Louisiana,	1023
Cincinnati, Ohio,	165	New York City, New York,	629
Cleveland, "	100	Niagara Falls, "	309
Columbus, "	45	New Haven, Connecticut,	676
Des Moines, Iowa,	679	Omaha, Nebraska,	813
Denver, Colorado,	1385	Peoria, Illinois,	414
Detroit, Michigan,	195	Philadelphia, Penn.,	539
Dayton, Ohio,	115	Pittsburg, "	185
Emporia, Kansas,	874	Quincy, Illinois,	544
Fort Scott, "	771	Richmond, Virginia,	495
Fort Wayne, Indiana,	168	Rock Island, Illinois,	505
Galveston, Texas,	1192	San Francisco, California,	2720
Houston, "	1143	Springfield, Illinois,	430
Harrisburg, Pennsylvania,	433	Springfield, Massachusetts,	684
Indianapolis, Indiana,	233	St. Joseph, Missouri,	750
Jacksonville, Florida,	1202	St. Louis, "	470
Jefferson, Missouri,	596	St. Paul, Minnesota,	768
Kansas City, "	745	Toledo, Ohio,	130
Keokuk, Iowa,	925	Topeka, Kansas,	813
Little Rock, Arkansas,	748	Vicksburg, Mississippi,	885
Leavenworth, Kansas,	770	Washington City, D. C.,	487
Lincoln, Nebraska,	853	Wheeling, W. Va.,	133
Lafayette, Indiana,	296	Wilmington, Delaware,	533
Louisville, Kentucky,	275	Worcester, Massachusetts,	738
Madison, Wisconsin,	497	Zanesville, Ohio,	50

Jewels in the English Crown.

Large Ruby,irreg'lar polish'd,	1	Brilliant Diamonds,	1,363
Large, broad spread Sapphire,	1	Rose Diamonds,	1,273
Sapphires,	16	Table Diamonds,	147
Emeralds,	11	Drop-shaped Pearls,	4
Rubies,	4	Pearls,	273

Total, - - - - - - - - - - - 3,093

5

A NOBLE PHYSICIAN.

BISHOP BEDELL, in an Address to a graduating medical class, dwells upon the influence of conscientiousness in a Physician. He gives the following interesting anecdote as an illustration of what he means by that moral quality:

"I was very ill in Chamounix, under the shadow of Mont Blanc. Those grand ice pinnacles, that majestic dome of snow, those slow-creeping glaciers, that brawling Arve, give to the valley—itself 4,000 feet above the sea level—an atmosphere which invalids resort to for health, and strong men for the luxury of breathing in. Men are not expected to be ill there.

"So there was no physician resident nearer than Geneva,—a long day's journey. But a physician had taken a house at Chamounix for the summer, waiting with his family until a lucrative situation, for which he had applied, should be open to him. He was in daily expectation of being summoned to his new home, when he was summoned to my bedside.

"He found a case of typhus fever. He watched and nursed me like a brother. During long weeks of semi-consciousness his presence met every moment of need. After about a month he received the welcome message that his new home was ready. He replied that he would come immediately, for his patient was recovering.

"But his patient relapsed. Again dangerous symptoms set in. And in the midst of them came a letter indicating that great anxiety existed for his presence at his new home. He asked for a little delay, expecting to be speedily relieved; but the symptoms were aggravated, and the disease unbroken.

"A telegram arrived, summoning him in a week. The week passed. He replied to it that his patient needed care a few days longer.

"He was not an unknown man. Trained in the Jesuit College at Turin, in the same class with Cavour, the great statesman of Italy, he devoted himself to medicine, and afterward taught it, in the medical Faculty of that city. During the Crimean war he was the head of a medical staff on the field. He had solicited the position which was now open to him, and had expected it anxiously. He was a devoted Roman Catholic, an Italian, having no ties nor any particular sympathy with an American and a Protestant.

"But his patient needed him. He stood between him and death. There was no one within a long day's journey to take that place. And, therefore, when the next telegram arrived, that he must come within twenty-four hours or the position would be given to another applicant, he calmly telegraphed in reply—his patient needed him. He would sacrifice the place, but not his duty.

"That was *conscientiousness*. And I write the name of CHARLES DUPRAZ high on the scroll of my grateful recollections of noble men—Physicians."

SPONTANEOUS COMBUSTION.

IT is now well known that many substances, under certain combinations, will take fire of themselves, upon the principle known as spontaneous combustion.

Cotton, saturated with linseed oil, has been known to inflame within two hours.

Canvass, painted with white lead and oil, dried, rolled, and put under cover, burned in a few hours.

An old packing sheet, smeared with oil, took fire.

Cotton Rags, on which oil had been spilled, took fire while being delivered from a cellar.

Dirty Rags, upon which workmen have wiped oil from their hands; these, thrown into a heap, are pretty sure to heat and ignite in time.

Linseed Oil, dropped upon wool, has caused several fires.

The paint and oil room of a carriage shop burst into a flame; cause, wood work smeared with flax seed oil.

Bituminous coal has burned spontaneously, and caused several large conflagrations.

Wool, greased for carding, ignited in a few hours.

Linen rags, in paper mills, undergoing fermentation, require careful attention.

A species of fireworks known as "red fire," purchased on the fourth of July, and not used, subsequently ignited and set fire to the house.

A man seated himself upon an empty oil barrel, which had been standing for some time upon the side walk, exposed to the sun. Wishing to light his pipe, he struck a match upon the barrel, when the gas, with which it was filled, exploded, severely injuring the temporary tenant.

BENEVOLENT INSTITUTIONS.

MASONIC.

MOUNT ZION LODGE, NO. 9.

CHARTER GRANTED, JANUARY 2, 1809.

First Located at Clinton, and removed to Mt. Vernon, April 5th, 1817, and organized in the Court House.

The first officers of the Lodge in 1809, were:

Samuel H. Smith,	W. M.	William F. Roberts,	S. D.
Alfred Manning,	S. W.	James Miller,	J. D.
Ichabod Nye,	J. W.	William Bartlett,)	Stewards.
Samuel Nye,	Treasurer.	Peter Wolf,)	
Oliver Strong,	Secretary.	Richard Fishback,	Tyler.

1810—First Representative to the Grand Lodge, S. H. Smith.

1814—The first Masonic Funeral in the county, was that of Richard Fishback, a merchant of Clinton, which took place on the 23d of May, 1814.

1876.——STATED MEETINGS.—Meets at Masonic Hall, N. E. Corner of Main and Vine streets, the *First Friday Evening of each Month*.

Present officers :

R. B. Marsh,	W. M.	O. G. Daniels,	Secretary.
William M. Koons,	S. W.	G. W. Sandford,	S. D.
Alexander Cassil,	J. W.	W. A. Crouch,	J. D.
Truman Ward,	Treasurer.	James R. Wallace,	Tyler.

——o——

CLINTON ROYAL ARCH CHAPTER, NO. 26.

Charter Granted, May 16, 1842.

The first officers were:

J. N. Burr,	E. H. P.	B. H. Taylor,	C. of H.
B. F. Smith,	King.	S. W. Burr,	R. A. C.
James Huntsberry,	Scribe.	A. Corbin,	
C. Delano,	P. S.	A. C. Rowland,	M. of Vails.
S. W. Burr,	Secretary.	J. Garrison,	
James Huntsberry,	Treasurer.	Joseph Muenscher,	Chaplain.

1876.——STATED MEETINGS.——Meets at Masonic Hall, the *Second Friday Evening of each Month*.

Present officers :

S. C. Thompson,	H. P.	G. W. Stahl,	Treasurer.
Alexander Cassil,	King.	S. H. Peterman,	Secretary.
Adam Harnwell,	Scribe.	W. B. Brown, G. M. of 3d Vail.
John F. Gay,	Capt. of Host.	E. M. Wright, G. M. of 2d Vail.
C. P. Gregory,	P. S.	J. W. Williams, G. M. of 1st Vail.
G. W. Sandford,	R. A. Capt.	James R. Wallace,	Guard.

CLINTON ENCAMPMENT, NO. 5, OF KNIGHT TEMPLARS AND APPENDANT ORDERS.

Charter Granted, October 12, 1843.

First officers:

Sir Joseph Muenscher,	E. Com.	Sir James Huntsberry,	Treas.
" B. F. Smith,	General.	" T. Winne,	Recorder.
" A. D. Bigelow,	Capt. Gen.	" A. Randolph,	Stnd. Bearer.
" J. N. Burr,	Prelate.	" Jos. Hildreth,	Swd. Bearer.
" C. Delano,	S. W.	" E. W. Cotton,	Warden.
" Isaac Davis,	J. W.	" D. D. Stevenson,	Sentinel.

1876.—STATED MEETINGS.—Meets at Masonic Hall, the *Third Friday Evening of each Month.*

Present officers:

Sir Alexander Cassil,	E. Com.	Sir W. B. Brown,	Treasurer.
" S. C. Thompson,	General.	" W. H. Barnes,	Recorder.
" O. G. Daniels,	Capt. Gen.	" H. Jaggers,	Swd. Bearer.
" O. M. Mulvany,	S. W.	" W. Sanderson,	Stnd. Bearer.
" William M. Koons,	J. W.	" G. W. Sandford,	Warden.
" C. P. Gregory,	Prelate.	" James R. Wallace,	Sentinel.

INDEPENDENT ORDER OF ODD FELLOWS.

—— o ——

MOUNT VERNON LODGE, NO. 20.

Instituted, June 21, 1843.

Charter Members—*Richard Blake, Liberty Waite, Lorenzo D. Nash, William Sullivan, Robert Wright.*

First officers:

Richard Blake,	N. G.	Lorenzo D. Nash,	Secretary.
Liberty Waite,	V. G.	William Sullivan,	Treasurer.

Initiated at the first meeting—John K. Miller, D. A. Robertson, James R. Wallace, Miller Moody, Matthew H. Mitchell, Thomas Winne.

Representatives to the Grand Lodge of Ohio: W. M. Bunn, R. C. Kirk, A. C. Elliott, John W. White, Henry Phillips, W. R. Hart.

1856.—William M. Bunn, Deputy Grand Master.

1876.—NIGHTS OF MEETING.—Meets in Hall No. 1, *Kremlin Block, every Wednesday Evening.*

Present officers:

R. M. Johnson,	N. G.	R. N. Kindrick,	Treasurer.
J. W. H. Tiffany,	V. G.	Edwin H. Brown,	I. G.
Charles F. Cochran,	Secretary.	John Y. Reeve,	O. G.
W. R. Hart,	Per. Sec'y.	William Mawer,	Sitting P. G.

QUINDARO LODGE, NO. 316.

Instituted, June 9, 1857.

Charter Members.—*G. B. Arnold, Joseph M. Byers, A. C. Elliott, J. F. Andrews, John Lamb, T. P. Fredrick, John Jennings.*

First officers:

Joseph M. Byers,	N. G.	A. C. Elliott,	Per. Sec'y.
T. P. Fredrick,	V. G.	J. F. Andrews,	Treasurer.
G. B. Arnold,	Secretary.		

Initiated at the first meeting—Israel Underwood, L. Munk.

Representatives to the Grand Lodge of Ohio—J. F. Andrews, Joseph M. Byers, T. P. Fredrick.

1876.—NIGHTS OF MEETING—Meets in Hall over J. W. Miller's store, *every Tuesday Evening.*

Present officers:

T. H. Trimble,	N. G.	George R. Martin,	Treasurer.
Joseph Hull,	V. G.	Alexander Coleman,	I. G.
D. W. Wood,	Per. Sec'y.	Samuel P. Weaver,	O. G.
George D. Neal,	Secretary.		

Max Leopold, District Deputy Grand Master, for Knox County.

——o——

KOKOSING ENCAMPMENT, NO. 38, I. O. O. F.

Instituted March 29, 1849.

Charter members—*I. M. Campbell, S. W. Gribbon, A. Ehle, L. G. Prentiss, R. C. Kirk, H. Phillips, A. P. Mather, V. Stevens.*

First officers:

I. M. Campbell,	C. P.	A. Ehle,	Scribe.
A. P. Mather,	H. P.	L. G. Prentiss,	Treasurer.
R. C. Kirk,	S. W.		

Initiated at first meeting—W. M. Bunn, J. A. Shannon, T. T. Tress, John Cooper, Robert B. Wright, John Eichelberger.

Representatives to the Grand Encampment of Ohio, since the adoption of the new Constitution in 1855—W. M. Bunn, John W. White, J. F. Andrews, Henry Phillips, W. R. Hart, A. C. Elliott, T. P. Fredrick.

1874-5—R. W. J. W. Grand Encampment—W. R. Hart.

1876.—NIGHTS OF MEETING—Meets in Hall No. 1, Kremlin Block, the *Second and Fourth Friday in each Month.*

Present officers:

William Mawer,	C. P.	Thomas Trick,	Scribe.
William R. Hart,	H. P.	George R. Martin,	Treasurer.
William H. Peoples,	S. W.	John Y. Reeve,	Sentinel.
Calvin Magers,	J. W.	Samuel P. Weaver,	P. C. P.

J. B. Warren, District Deputy Grand Patriarch.

KNIGHTS OF PYTHIAS.

—— o ——

"TIMON LODGE, NO. 45,"

Was Instituted on the 18th day of April, 1872.

The first officers were:

W. A. Crouch,	C. C.	William T. Elwell,	M. of F.
J. Monroe Hill,	V. C.	Henry H. King,	M. at A.
Richard F. West,	Prelate.	William B. Norton,	I. G.
Edward Vincent, K. of R. & S.		Samuel P. Weaver,	O. G.
John M. Armstrong, M. of E.			

The following are the Past Chancellors since the organization :

1872—Richard F. West, W. A. Crouch and J. Monroe Hill.
1873—Henry H. King and W. A. Crouch.
1874—John H. Stevens and John D. Haymes.
1875—R. B. Bingham and Samuel H. Peterman.

1876.——NIGHTS OF MEETING—Meets *every Thursday Evening,* in Quindaro Hall, South Main Street.

Present officers :

S. C. Thompson,	P. C.	John H. Stevens,	M. of E.
William Appleton,	C. C.	T. H. Trimble,	M. of F.
Leroy G. Hunt,	V. C.	R. B. Bingham,	M. at A.
J. W. H. Tiffany,	Prelate.	U. O. Stevens,	I. G.
W. A. Crouch,	K. of R. S.	Samuel P. Weaver,	O. G.

Representative to the Grand Lodge—John H. Stevens.

—— + —— ·

IMPROVED ORDER OF RED MEN.

—— o ——

MOHICAN TRIBE, NO. 69, I. O. R. M.

Instituted 18th Sun, Hot Moon, G. S. D 381, (June 18, 1872.)

First Chiefs :

W. R. Hart,	Sachem.	W. F. Gantt, K. of Wampum.
H. Graff,	Sen. Sagamore.	J. C. Gordon,	Sannap.
F. S. Crowell, Jun.	"	J. Clayton,	G. of Wigwam.
S. C. Thompson,	Prophet.	R. M. Johnson,	G. of Forest.
J. B. Warren, Chief of Records.			

1875—G. J. Sagamore—*William R. Hart.*
1875—Representative to Great Council—*H. Graff.*
1876—   "   "   "   *S. C. Thompson.*

1876.——NIGHTS OF MEETING——Meets *every Monday Evening,* at their Wigwam, Third Story of Sperry's Block, South-West Side of Public Square .

Present Chiefs:

Joseph C. Gordon, Sachem.
R. M. Johnson, Sen. Sagamore.
T. H. Trimble, Jun. "
A. Vance, Prophet.
W. A. Crouch, Chief of Records.

W. Cochran, K. of Wampum.
W. R. Hart, Sannap.
W. Sanderson, G. of Wigwam.
A. March, G. of Forest.

CATHOLIC BENEVOLENT ASSOCIATION.

——o——

ST. VINCENT DE PAUL BENEVOLENT SOCIETY.

Organized, August —, 1873.

First officers:

John Henegan, President.
C. O'Boyle, Vice President.

John Lawler, Secretary.
Dennis Corcoran, Treasurer.

1876.——TIME OF MEETING—*Semi-Monthly—Thursday Evenings.*—Hall, Third Story Weaver's Building, over Errett's Tin Ware and Stove Establishment, South Main Street, one door north of Dr. Green's Drug Store.

Present officers:

John Lawler, President.
James Britt, Vice President.

Michael Lee, Secretary.
J. H. Milless, Treasurer.

KNIGHTS OF HONOR.

——o——

KNOX LODGE, NO. 31, K. OF H.

Organized, October 1, 1874.

First officers:

S. C. Thompson, Past Dictator,
H. Graff, Dictator.
S. L. Baker, Vice Dictator.
W. Sanderson, Jr. Asst. "
J. F. Myers, Guide.

W. W. McKay, Reporter.
W. Cochran, Financial "
A. Vance, Treasurer.
S. Wright, Sentinel.

1876.——NIGHTS OF MEETING—*Every Wednesday Evening.*—Hall, Third Floor Sperry's Block, south-west side Public Square.

Present officers:

J. F. Myers, Past Dictator.
J. W. Tousley, Dictator.
John N. Myers, Vice Dictator.
D. W. Agnew, Asst. Dictator.
Hezekiah Graff, Chaplain.
W. T. Critchfield, Guide.

C. A. Merriman, Reporter.
R. C. Mitchell, Financial "
S. L. Baker, Treasurer.
Henry Cooper, Guardian.
G. B. Selby, Sentinel.

SONS OF TEMPERANCE.

— o —

MOUNT VERNON DIVISION, NO. 108.

Re-Organized, Feb. 16, 1876.

First officers :

Bro. H. Graff,	W. P.	Sister Jennie Hurlburt,	W. C.
Sister Alvira Lane,	W. A. P.	Bro. Wm. Cochran,	W. Condr.
Bro. L. B. Farish,	W. R. S.	Sister Katie Martin,	W. A. C.
Sister Anna Evans,	W. A. S.	" Jennie Chapman,	W. I. S.
Bro. J. H. Branyan,	W. F. S.	Bro. James A. Lane,	W. O. S.
" E. H. Briggs,	W. Treas.	" Wm. Cochran,	Deputy.

1876.—NIGHTS OF MEETING—Meets in Hall No. 2, Kremlin Block, *every Friday Evening.*

Present officers :

Bro. Wm. Cochran,	W. P.	Bro. Charles Beach,	W. Condr.
Sister Jennie Hurlburt,	W. A. P.	Sister M. Marshall,	W. A. C.
Bro. Frank Graff,	W. R. S.	" R. Tilson,	W. I. S.
Sister Eva Graff,	W. A. S.	Bro. Frank Wealey,	W. O. S.
Bro. W. Craig,	W. F. S.	" J. H. Branyan,	W. P. P.
" E. H. Briggs,	W. Treas.	" Wm. Cochran,	Deputy.

MEDICAL SOCIETY.

— o —

KNOX COUNTY MEDICAL SOCIETY.

Organized, May 2, 1863.

First officers :

President—Dr. B. W. PUMPHREY, Mount Vernon.
First Vice President—Dr. C. E. Bryant,   "
Second   "   "   Dr. J. W. Russell, Sr.,   "
Secretary—Dr. Matthew Thompson,   "
Treasurer—Dr. S. T. Bourne, Gambier.

1876.—Present officers :

President—Dr. S. C. POTTER, Fredericktown.
First Vice President—Dr. C. Sapp, Gambier.
Second   "   "   Dr. T. B. Wiser, Martinsburgh.
Secretary—Dr. J. W. McMillen, Mount Vernon.
Treasurer—Dr. P. Pickard,   "
Board of Examiners—Drs. J. W. Russell, S. B. Potter,
B. W. Pumphrey, F. C. Larimore and J. N. Burr.

6

FIRE INSURANCE COMPANY.

— o —

KNOX COUNTY MUTUAL INSURANCE COMPANY,

OF MOUNT VERNON. OHIO

Chartered in 1838—(Perpetual)—Commenced Business, August,1839.

First officers:

President—C. P. BUCKINGHAM.

Secretary—Samuel J. Updegraff.

Treasurer—E. G. Woodward.

—DIRECTORS.—

C. P. Buckingham,	C. Delano,
H. B. Curtis,	B. S. Brown,
George Browning,	Eli Miller,
J. E. Davidson,	Isaac Hadley.
S. J. Updegraff,	

1876.——Present officers:

President—JARED SPERRY.

Secretary and Treasurer—William Turner.

General Agent and Adjuster—S. L. Taylor.

—DIRECTORS.—

Jared Sperry,	Robert Thompson,
William McClelland,	S. L. Taylor,
H. H. Greer,	N. N. Hill,
Charles Cooper,	Thomas Odbert.
Joseph M. Byers,	

OFFICE.—East High Street, South Side, nearly opposite the Court House.

LIFE INSURANCE COMPANY.

— o —

THE CITIZENS' MUTUAL LIFE & HEALTH INSURANCE COMPANY,

OF MOUNT VERNON. OHIO.

ORGANIZED, JULY 31, 1869.

First officers:

President—Judge JOSEPH S. DAVIS.

Vice President—Judge John Adams.

Secretary and Treasurer—John W. White.

—DIRECTORS.—

Joseph S. Davis,	Joseph Watson,
John Adams,	George R. Martin.
Israel Green,	

1876.——Present officers:

President—Judge JOSEPH S. DAVIS.
Vice President—Judge John Adams.
Secretary—J. J. Fultz.
Treasurer—R. N. Kindrick.
Legal Adviser—David C. Montgomery.
Medical Directors—S. C. Thompson, M. D.,
Israel Bedell, M. D.

—DIRECTORS.—

Hon. John D. Thompson, Treasurer C. Mt. V. & C. R.R.
Hon. George W. Morgan, ex-Member of Congress.
Prof. R. B. Marsh, Supt. Schools, Mount Vernon, Ohio.
John Adams, Judge Court Common Pleas.
T. P. Fredrick, Mayor City Mount Vernon, Ohio.
Joseph S. Davis, ex-Probate Judge Knox County, Ohio.
Calvin Magers, City Marshal.
John Ponting, Merchant.
George W. Bunn, General Superintendent & Contractor.

J. J. FULTZ, General Agent.

Office—Office with D. C. MONTGOMERY, *Attorney at Law*, N.
W. Corner Main Street and Public Square, MOUNT VERNON, O.

COUNTY AGRICULTURAL SOCIETY.

——o——

Records of the proceedings of the first Agricultural Fairs held in Knox County, I have utterly failed to unearth,—not even the preliminary steps taken to effect an organization can be obtained at this date. This should not be the case, and I trust that all future officers of this important county Association, and more particularly the Secretaries, will see that a fair and impartial record of every transaction of the Society is placed upon the proper minute book.

The first Knox County Fair that I have any recollection of, was held, I believe, in 1852 or 1853. The display made was nothing to brag of. The Court Room of the Court House, then standing on the north-west quarter of the Public Square, was made use of for an Art Hall. Mr. A. Ban. Norton took prominent part in its management—either as its President or Secretary.

The officers of the Society for 1876, are:

President—Alexander Cassil.
Vice President—Peres Critchfield.
Secretary—Willard S. Hyde.
Treasurer—Ira M. McFarland.
Board of Directors—Clinton Township, two members.
Other Townships, one each.

Fair, 1876.—September 26th, 27th, 28th, and 29th.

SCHOOL DEPARTMENT.

—o—

BOARD OF EDUCATION.

Joseph S. Davis,   President. | Hezekiah Graff,   Member.
A. R. McIntire,   Secretary. | William B. Russell,   "
W. P. Bogardus,   Treasurer. | Benjamin Grant,   "

MOUNT VERNON HIGH SCHOOL.

Prof. R. B. MARSH, A. M., SUPERINTENDENT.

Mr. J. H. Richards,   Teacher. | Miss Ermina J. Day, Teacher.

GRAMMAR.

Miss Letitia S. Elder,   No. 1. | Miss Anna B. McMillen, No. 2.

SECONDARIES.

Miss V. E. Fawcett,   No. 4. | Miss Callie White,   No. 2.
"   Emma J. Trimble, "   3. | "   Maria L. Fawcett, "   1.

INTERMEDIATE.

Miss Sylvia Mount,   No. 4. | Miss Lena K. Hodgins, No. 1.
"   Bessie Wells,   "   3. |

PRIMARIES.

Miss Mary Devoe,   No. 5. | Miss Clara M. White,   No. 2.
"   Anna Mead,   "   4. | "   Fannie Blanchard, "   1.
"   Frank A. Hood,   "   3. |

PAROCHIAL SCHOOL.

—o—

ST. VINCENT DE PAUL'S PAROCHIAL SCHOOL.

UNDER THE SUPERVISION OF FATHER BRENT.

TEACHERS—SISTER JOHNS,   )   OF
              SISTER THERESSA,) SAINT FRANCES.

SCHOOL HOUSES.

UNION SCHOOL BUILDING, N. W. Corner Mulberry and
    Hamtramck Streets.
FIRST WARD SCHOOL HOUSE, north side Front Street,
    between McKenzie and McArthur Streets.
SECOND WARD SCHOOL HOUSE, north side west Gam-
    bier Street, between Walnut and West Streets.
THIRD WARD SCHOOL HOUSE, north side Chestnut
    Street, between Gay and McKenzie Streets.
FOURTH WARD SCHOOL HOUSE, south side west Sugar
    Street, between West and Norton Streets.
FIFTH WARD SCHOOL HOUSE, west Plimpton Street.
*SAINT VINCENT DE PAUL'S PAROCHIAL SCHOOL
    HOUSE*, north-east corner of High and McKenzie Streets.

Church Directory.

——— o ———

HOURS OF DIVINE SERVICE:

SUNDAYS—10½ o'clock, A. M., Summer, 7½ o'clock, P. M.
Winter, 7 o'clock, P. M.
THURSDAY EVENING PRAYER MEETINGS—Summer,
7½ o'clock, P. M.—Winter, 7 o'clock, P. M.

——— o ———

ASSOCIATED REFORM PRESBYTERIAN CHURCH—
North Main street, west side, north-west corner Main and Sugar.
Pulpit vacant.

AFRICAN METHODIST CHURCH—West Front street,
south side. Rev. D. N. Mason.

BAPTIST CHURCH—West Vine street, between Mulberry
and Mechanic. Rev. F. M. Iams.

CONGREGATIONAL CHURCH—North Main street, north-
east corner Main and Sugar. Rev. E. B. Burrows.

CHRISTIAN CHURCH—East Vine street, south side, between Gay and McKenzie. Rev. Leonard Southmayd.

EVANGELICAL LUTHERAN CHURCH—North Sandus-
ky street, west side, between High and Sugar. Pulpit vacant.

METHODIST EPISCOPAL CHURCH—North Gay street,
south-east corner of Gay and Chestnut. Rev. G. W. Pepper.

METHODIST CHURCH—North Mulberry street, west side,
between Sugar and Hamtramck. Rev. J. A. Thrap.

OWL CREEK BAPTIST CHURCH, Morgan township.—
Rev. A. J. Wiant. Rev. Wiant's residence is on e Vine street.
Mount Vernon, Ohio.

PRESBYTERIAN CHURCH—North Gay street, east side,
north-east corner Gay and Chestnut.. Rev. O. H. Newton.

PROTESTANT EPISCOPAL CHURCH—East High street,
north side, north-east corner High and Gay. Rev. William
Thompson.

SAINT VINCENT DE PAUL'S CHURCH,—[Catholic.]
East High street, north side, north-east corner of High and Mc-
Kenzie. Father Brent. Hours of service—Daily, (Sundays
excepted) at 7 o'clock, A. M. Sunday, at 10 o'clock, A. M., and
3 o'clock P. M.

Directory For 1876--7.

A

	Popu-lation.		Minors	
	M	F	M	F
ANDREWS, JAMES M., Grocer, south Main, residence east Front street, - - - -	2	4	1	3
Andrews, Ella, residence east Front.				
Andrews, Orriette, " " "				
Andrews, Hattie, " " "				
Andrews, James Frank, " "				
ANDREWS, JOHN M., Attorney, No. 2, Kremlin, (up stairs,) res Columbus road.				
Andrews, Alice, " "				
Andrews, Florence, " "				
Andrews, William N., Farmer, res Columbus road				
ADAMS, JOHN, Judge Court Common Pleas, residence n e corner Gay and Front street.	2	4	1	3
Adams, Anna, " " "				
Adams, Frances, " " "				
Adams, Philip Burr, " " "				
Adams, Joseph, residence Coshocton road.				
Adams, George, wagon maker, res east Front st.	1	1		
Adams, Mrs. Hester, residence east Gambier st.		2		
Adams, Arthur A., blacksmith, south Mulberry, residence west Front st. - - - -	1	2		1
Adams & Rogers, dealers in Iron, Nails, &c. Pub Sqr				

Our Agency does a GENERAL FIRE, LIFE and ACCIDENT BUSINESS.	Population.		Minors.	
	M	F	M	F
ADAMS, ADAM, (A. & Rogers,) Iron merchant Public Square, residence west Sugar street.	2	3	1	2
Adams, Sadie, residence west Sugar street.				
Adams, Emma, " " "				
Adams, William, laborer, res " " "	1			
Adams, James, blacksmith, res north Main street.	1	2		1
Adams, Mrs. Ellen, res corner Main and Pleasant.		2		
Abbott, Mrs. Ellen, res s w cor Gay and Front sts.		1		
Abbott, Cornelius C., farmer, "	1			
Abbott, John S., Farmer, res Clinton township.				
Albert, Samuel, carpenter, res Oak & Rogers sts.	2	2	1	1
Albert, Aaron, " res east Gambier st.	1			
Albert, Alexander, laborer, res new Gambier road.	3	1	2	
Agnew, D. W., Clerk, res east Lamartin street.	2	3	1	
Agnew, Mrs. D. W., milliner, s Main, res Lamartin				
Agnew, Mary A., " " "				
Agnew, Sarah, " " "				
Aker, Mrs. R., brds with L. H. Lewis, e Burgess.		1		
Allen, Wm. P., Agr'al Impl'ts, bds Bergin House.	1	1		
Allen, Peter, Flanger, res east Chestnut street.	3	2	2	1
Allen, Asahel, farmer, residence Columbus road.				
Allen, Salome, boards with Dr. Burr, e High st.		1		
Armstrong, Mrs. Margaret, res north Gay street.		2		
Armstrong, Hattie, " " "				
ARMSTRONG, JOHN M., Sheriff Knox County, residence south side east Chestnut street.	1			
Armstrong, E., carpenter, residence east High st.	1	1		
Armstrong, G. W., " res east Chestnut st.	1	1		
Armstrong & Tilton, Family Grocers, south Main.				
ARMSTRONG, J. C., (of the firm of A. & Tilton) residence east High street. - - - -	2	1	1	
Armstrong, Charles, machinist, res west Gambier.	1	1		
Arentrue, Mrs. John, res Gambier and McKenzie.		1		
Arentrue, Jane, " " "		1		
Ault, John Sebastian, carpenter, res east Front st.	3	3	2	2
Altaffer, John, Cdr C. Mt. V. & C. RR., res e Front.	2	3	1	2
Allison, Frank, painter, residence south Gay st.	2	1	1	
Allison, J. M., finisher cab. ware, bds Mrs Ewalts.	1			
Ashton, Philip, laborer, res Wooster Avenue. -	1	1		
Ashton, Josiah, Poney Express, res north Gay st.	1	2		1
Ardner, Mrs. Hannah, residence north Gay street.	2	3	2	
Ashford, E. S., wagon maker, res Wooster Ave.	1	1		
ARNOLD, O. M., dealer in Queensware & Fancy Goods, south Main, res cor Main & Plimpton.	4	2	3	
ATWOOD, HARRISON, Real Estate Agent, residence Wooster Avenue. - - - -	1	2		
Atwood, Abby, residence Wooster Avenue.				
Atwood, William, brick mason, " "	1			

Fire Policies issued from one to five years, by *J. J. Fultz.*	Popu lation.		Minors.	
	M	F	M	F
Atwood, Ira, harness maker, res s Mulberry st.	1			
Alsdorf & Patterson, lumber dealers, w Gambier.				
ALSDORF, JAMES R., (of the above firm,) residence s w corner High and West streets.	2	4	1	3
Aldine Job Printing Office, corner Main and Vine.				
Ash, Chambers, farmer, residence Newark road.				
Anderson, J. A., (A. & Stallo,) furniture dealer, s Main, residence n w cor Sugar and West.	1	1		
Anderson, D. W., farmer, residence e High street.	1	2		
Anderson, T. M., carpenter & teacher, " "	1			
Anderson, Robt. C., " " " "	1			
Allam, William, machinist, residence cor Norton and Hamtramck streets. - - - -	1	1		
Alling, Wm. H., grocer, near B. & O. RR., residence west Sugar street. - - - -	1	2		1
Allspaugh, Henry, coal dealer, res west Chestnut.	2	1	1	
Allspaugh, Fillmore, laborer, " "	1			
Allspaugh, George, " res Sandusky st.	1	2		1
Austin, Daniel, [c] " res east High street.	1			
Antrican, Jeremiah, tanner, residence west Vine.	1	3		2
Atherton, John, carpenter, residence west High.	1			
Atherton, Mrs. ——, residence west Vine street.		1		
Appleton, Wm., carpenter, residence west High.	2	1	1	
Adler Brothers, clothiers, south Main street.				
Adler, Moses, (of the above firm,) brds west High.	1			
Ammadon, Wm., plasterer, brds Central House.	1			

B

BALDWIN, W. F., hatter and furrier, s Main, residence in W. L. King's block, s Main st.	2	2	1	1
Baldwin, Hattie, teacher, res " "		1		
Baldwin, Maggie V., postal clerk, res "		1		
BALDWIN, Charles F., asst. supt. P. C. & St. L. R. R., residence east Gambier Street. - -	1	1		1
Baldwin, Henry, tinner, res Columbus road.				
Back, James, carpenter, res rear of Savings Bank.	2	5	1	4
Beach, A. J., ex-sheriff, residence e Gambier st.	1	1		
Beach, S. O., cab. maker, res cor West & Chestnut.	2	4	1	3
Beach, James, farmer, " " "	1			
Beach, Rollin, " residence Columbus road.				
Beach, Mary J., seamstress, boards with John C. Davis, west Burgess street. - - - -		1		
Beach, Mrs. Mary, res cor Mulberry & Chestnut.		1		
Beckley, Henry, farmer, res Pleasant township.				
Butler, S. J., book keeper & ins. agt, res w Sugar.	1	1		

7

THE

Zanesville Weekly Signal.

A FAMILY NEWSPAPER,

DEVOTED TO

INSTRUCTIVE AND ENTERTAINING READING,

LITERATURE, PUBLIC AFFAIRS, GENERAL AND LOCAL INTELLIGENCE, THE ADVANCEMENT OF HOME INTERESTS, &C.

Democratic and Liberal in Politics.

PUBLISHED EVERY WEEK,

At the Rate of $2.00 a Year, in Advance.

OFFICE NORTH-WEST CORNER MAIN AND FOURTH STREET, THIRD STORY. ENTRANCE ON FOURTH STREET, OPPOSITE COURT HOUSE.

JAMES T. IRVINE,
Editor and Publisher.

ZANESVILLE, OHIO, 1876.

Call and get our Rates before Insuring elsewhere.	Population.		Minors.	
	M	F	M	F
Bassett, Jean, cabinet maker and carver, poncy express and bill poster, res w Chestnut st. -	1	2		1
BANNER JOB PRINTING OFFICE, s w cor Main and Gambier streets.				
Boynton Henry, fireman, C. Mt. V. & C. R. R., residence east Front street. - - - -	1	1		
Boynton, LeGrand, clerk, res east Chestnut street.	1			
BOYNTON, NOAH, ex-postmaster, residence east Chestnut street. - - - - -	3	2	2	
BERGIN HOUSE, (T. McBride & Son, proprietors,) south-west cor Main & Front streets.				
Bergin, Brian, policeman, res east Burgess street.	1	1		
Bergin, William, residence east Vine street. -	1	1		
Bergin, William, Jr., clerk, res " " -	1			
Bergin, Dana, tinner, " " "	1			
Bergin, Clara A., " " " -		1		
Bergin, Thurlow, residence south Main street. -	1			
Beeman, Samuel, commissioner, res Ankneytown				
Berger, Samuel, miller, res south Main street. -	1	3		1
Berger, Nettie, " " " "				
BURR, Dr. J. N., physician and surgeon, residence south-east cor High & McKenzie streets.	1	2		1
Burr, Thomas J., " " "	1			
Bechtol, Charles, carpenter, res east Chestnut st.	3	2	2	
Bechtol, William, " " "				
Bechtol, Ella, " " "				
BECHTOL, JOHN, brewer, Center Run, residence Center Run.				
Bechtol, Joseph, butcher, res Pleasant township.				
Baker, C. S. J., restaurant w High, nr B. & O. RR	2	1	1	
Baker Brothers, druggists, south Main street.				
BAKER, GEO. R., (of Baker Bros.) druggist, residence east Front street. - - -	2	2	1	
BAKER, SAMUEL LEWIS, (of Baker Bros.) druggist, residence west Vine street. -	3	2	2	1
Baker, Joseph, laborer, res Coshocton avenue. -	2	5	1	2
BARKER, JOSEPH N., barber, Woodward Opera House, residence north Main street. -	2	2	1	1
Bennett, Mrs. Mary, residence south Norton st. -	1	4	1	3
Bennett, Clara, " " "		1		
Bennett, Alice, " west High st. -		1		
Bennett, C. L., livery, w Gambier, res n Gay st. -	2	2	1	1
Bennett, George S., dentist, " " -	1			
Bennett, Murray J., painter, " " -	1			
Bennett, Henry P., grocer, near Public Square, residence north Main street. - - -	2	1	1	
Bennett, Norman, plasterer, res north Gay street.	2	1	1	
Bennett, Amos, laborer, " " -	1	2		1

CHRONOLOGISTS' THEORIES ON DATE OF CREATION.

	B. C.
The Hebrew Text, according to Moreri, gives it as -	4,003
Usher, generally adopted by the English, - - -	4,004
The Septuagint, according to Riccioli, - - -	5,634
The Vulgate, according to Riccioli, - - -	4,184
Petavius, in Strauchius, - - - - - - -	3,983
The Benedictines, in the Art of Verifying Dates, - -	4,963

Ninety million people speak the English language.
Seventy-five million   "   German   "
Fifty-five   "   "   Spanish   "
Forty-five   "   "   French   "

THE FIVE AGES.

The Golden, or Patriarchal, under the care of Saturn.
The Silver, " Voluptuous, "   "   Jupiter.
The Brazen, " Warlike, "   "   Neptune.
The Heroic, " Rennaissant, "   "   Mars.
The Iron, " Present, "   "   Pluto.

PARAGRAPHS.

1.—There are 2,750 languages.
2.—Two persons die every second.
3.—The Average of human life is 31 years.

	Popu-lation.		Miners	
Mutual Fire Companies a Special-ty. **J. J. FULTZ,** *Agent.*	M	F	M	F
Bennett, Mrs. Margaret, res cor High & Harrison.	·	1		
Bennett, James, laborer, residence e Chestnut st.	1	4		2
Banning, Mrs. J. S., res Chesterville road.				
Banning, Thomas, " "				
Banning, Anthony, res s w cor High & Mechanic.	2	1	1	
Banning, William, (of the firm of McCormick, Willis & B.) res s w cor High & Mechanic sts	1			
Banning, George, " "		1		
Banning, William D., farmer, res Clinton tp.				
Banning, J. Blackstone, " res Mansfield road.				
Bray, N. L., [c] barber, Kirk hall, res n Gay st. -	3	1	2	
Barnes, Henry, res north Gay street. - -	1	1		
Barnes, W. H., ins. agent, res north Main street.	4	6	3	3
Barnes, Jennie, brds with N. N. Hill, "		1		
Barry, Mrs. Mary, brds with Jno. Henegan, e High		1		
Benedict, Heman, clerk, res n Mulberry street. -	1	2		1
Benedict, Catharine, " "				
Benedict, Carla, teacher, " " -		1		
Boyd, Mrs. Ellen, " "		3		
Boyd, John, township trustee, res s Mulberry st. -	1	2		
Boyd, Maggie A., music teacher, "		1		
Boyd, Sadie E., "				
Boyd, George W., huckster, "	1	1		1
Boyd, Almeda, residence west Chestnut street. -		1		
Boyd & McConnell, dealers in glass ware, tin ware and notions, cor Gay and Gambier streets.				
BOYD, JOHN B., (of the above firm,) residence west High street. - - - -	1	1		
Boyd, Miss M. J., telegraph operator, res w High.		1		
Bunn, William M., painter, res e Chestnut street.	1	1		
BUNN, GEORGE W., painter and glazier, residence east Chestnut street. - - -	4	3	3	1
Bunn, George B., watchmaker, res e Chestnut st.				
Bunn, John R., painter, " " -	1			
Bunn, Frank N., " " " -	2		1	
BUNN, ALBERT D., produce dealer, north Mulberry, residence north Mulberry street, - -	1	3		2
Bunn, Alden S., painter, brds Central House, -	1			
Bimrick, W. J., cutter, res west Chesnut street. -	1	2		1
Bartholemew, Wm., barber, brds Central House.	1			
BRENT, JULIUS, Catholic Priest, residence s e corner Chestnut and McKenzie street. - -	2		1	
Brent, Fanny, " " " -		1		
Brent & Rogers, grain and flour dealers, Norton's old stand, near B. & O. R. R. depot.				
Brent Sam'l. J., (of the above firm,) res e Front.	1	6		4
Brent, E. V. ex-probate judge, res w Sugar street.	2	2	1	
Brent, Alice, " "		1		

NEW
SADDLE & HARNESS SHOP.

HAVING sold my interest in the Shop on the Public Square, I have opened a

NEW SHOP ON SOUTH MAIN STREET,

Three Doors North Rowley House,

Where I will be happy to see all my old friends of Knox county that have stood by me. *MY EXPENSES ARE VERY LIGHT*, consequently I can sell very low for *Cash or Ready Pay.*

REPAIRING OF ALL KINDS

Promptly attended to. *PLEASE GIVE ME A CALL.*

WILLIAM M. THOMPSON.

Mount Vernon, Ohio, 1876.

Empty oil barrels, when subjected to heat, or left standing in the sun, will generate and become filled with gas, which is liable to explosion if a light is brought near it. Some years ago, an oil barrel, which had been empty for three years, standing in the cellar of Taylor's Saloon, New York, was approached with a light by one of the porters, when a violent explosion occurred, setting fire to the building.

CUBIC MEASURE.

A Cubic foot has 1728 inches.

An Ale gallon has 282 cubic inches.

A Wine gallon has 231 cubic inches.

A Dry gallon has 268 8-10 cubic inches.

A Bushel has 2,150 4-10 cubic inches.

A Cord of Wood has 128 cubic feet.

A Ton of Round Timber has 50 cubic feet.

A Ton of Hewn Timber has 40 cubic feet.

A pile of Wood 4 ft. high, 4 ft. broad, and 8 ft. long, makes one cord.

A box 24x16 inches, 22 inches deep, contains one barrel.

A box 16x16½ inches, 8 inches deep, contains one bushel.

A box 8x8½ inches, 8 inches deep, contains one peck.

A box 4x4 inches, 4½ inches deep, contains a half peck.

A box 4x3 inches, 2½ inches deep, contains one quart.

Insurance on Dwellings and Contents a Specialty.

	Population.		Minors.	
	M	F	M	F
Brent, Walter, student, residence w Sugar street.				
Blocher, George, carpenter, res Oak street.	5	2	4	1
Blocher, John M., clerk express office, res e Gambier street.	3	3	2	2
Blocher, Jacob, blacksmith, res e Gambier street.	1	1		
Blocher, Mrs. Rebecca. " " "	1	1	1	
BURKE, P. H., ticket and freight agent, Baltimore & Ohio Railroad, boards Bergin House.	1			
Burke, James, teamster, res e Hamtramck st.	1	1		
Pooze, Mrs. Eliza, boarding house, s Mulberry st.		2		
Pooze, Jacob, farmer, res south Harrison street.	1	1		
Bishop's Grain Ware House, Woodbridge's old stand, west Gambier street.				
BISHOP, SAMUEL, grain dealer, Woodbridge's old ware house, residence Newark road.				
Bishop, Porter, boiler maker, res east Front street.	2	4	1	3
Bishop, Emma, " "		1		
Bishop, Cena, " "				
Bedell, Israel, physician, n Main, res w Chestnut.	1	2		1
Bedell, J. E., grocer, s Main, res High & Harrison	4	1	3	
Bedell, Mrs. Mary, " "		1		
Bedell, Raymond, grocer, s Main, res west Vine.	1	1		
Beam, Mrs. Martha, residence n Mulberry street.	1	3	1	2
Beam, Belle, " "				
Beam, Clara, " "				
Beam, Frank L., clerk, " "				
BEAM, WILLIAM, insurance agent, residence n w cor Mulberry and Chestnut sts.	1	3		
Beam, Samantha, res " "				
Beam, Louisa, " "				
Baughman, John, butcher, res s Mulberry street.	1			
Barncard, George, cooper, " "	2	2	1	1
Brown, Miss Nannie, res east Gambier street.		3		
Brown, John, machinist, res west Chestnut st.	1			
Brown, Edwin H., machinist, res n West street.	1	3		2
Brown, S. L., "Indian Doctor," res Railroad st.	1	1		1
Brown, Benjamin B., residence Chester street.	1	1		
Brown, Mrs. S. L., residence east Chestnut st.		1		
Brown, Ada, teacher, "		1		
BROWN, WILLIAM B., jeweler, s Main st. residence corner Scott and Mulberry sts.	3	2	2	1
Byers & Bird, dealers in general hardware, west side south Main street.				
BYERS, JOSEPH M., (of the above firm,) residence n e cor Gay and Vine streets.	2	1	1	
Byers, Elizabeth, " " "		1		
Byers, Mrs. Elizabeth, " " "		1		
Byers, Maggie, " " "		1		

NATIONAL COLORS.

United States—-Stars on blue and white, with red stripes.
Great Britain—Red and blue.
Austria—Red and white.
Bavaria—White, bordered with blue.
Denmark—Red.
France—Blue, white and red.

Netherlands--Red, white & blue
Portugal—White, border'd with red.
Russia—Yellow.
Spain—Red and white.
Sweden—Blue, bordered with yellow.
Switzerland—Red.

THE SYMBOLISMS OF COLOR.

Black ⎫
Brown ⎬ —Death and sorrow.
Green—Fickleness.
Blue—Constancy.

White—Purity.
Yellow—Jealousy.
Purple—Royalty.

IN RAILWAY SIGNALS.

Red, Danger.   Green, Caution.   White, Clear or safe.

A TABLE OF DISTANCES.

An acre contains 4,840 square yards.
209 ft. long by 209 ft. broad is 1 acre.
A mile is 5,280 ft. or 1,760 yds.
A league is 3 miles.

A fathom is 6 feet.
A cubic is 2 feet.
A hand is 4 inches.
A palm is 3 inches.
A space is 3 feet.
A span is 10½ inches.

Insure against Fire and Lightning. *J. J. Fultz, Agt.*	Popula- tion.		Minors.	
	M	F	M	F
Bricker, James, laborer, res Coshocton avenue. -	3	2	2	1
Bricker, David, " res Railroad street. -	1	1		
Bricker, Cynthia, residence north Mulberry st. -		1		
Bourner, Benjamin, laborer, res near s Harrison st.	1	1		
Broadhurst, William, residence west Vine street.	2	2	1	
Bair, Simon H., cigar maker, res High & Walnut.	5	2	4	1
Bixby, David, res corner High & Adams streets. -	1	1		
Bixby, Henry, machinist, res cor Sugar & West. -	3	1	2	
Bixby, Belle, " " "				
Blair, Zohar, mill-wright, res Adams & Chestnut.	1	4		2
Blair, Joseph, pattern maker, " " -	1			
Blair, Jesse, carpenter, res n Mulberry street. -	1	2		1
Blair, T. M., engr. C. Mt. V. & C. R.R., boards at				
Rowley House. - - - - - -	1			
Bell, Joseph G., Round House C. Mt. V. & C. R.R.				
residence corner Chestnut & Catharine sts. -	2	2	1	1
Berry, Belle, [c] res cor Chestnut & Mulberry sts.		1		
BRADDOCK, JOHN S., real estate agent,				
post office building, res 189 w High street.	3	3	2	1
Bradford, Alexander, machinist, res s Norton st.	1	3		2
Barr, Allen, laborer, residence east High street. -	1	1		
Barr, Mrs. Lydia, seamstress, res w Vine street.		1		
Barr, Hannah, " " " " -		1		
Barr, Samuel, druggist, " " -	1			
Barr, Franklin, blacksmith, " east High st.	1	2		1
Barrett, Patrick, teamster, " e Chestnut st.	3	3	2	2
Barrett, John, laborer, res e Plimpton street. -	1	1		
Browning & Sperry, dealers in dry goods, notions,				
&c., south Main street, west side.				
BROWNING, W. D., (of the above firm,) resi-				
dence south Gay street. - - - - -	2	2	1	1
Browning, Mrs., boards with W. D. Browning. -		1		
Brock, William, gardner, res Center Run.				
Boyle, Michael, Sr., plasterer, res e High street.	2	1	1	
Boyle, Michael, Jr., " " " -	1			
Boyle, John, " " " -	1			
Boyle, Harry, pattern maker, res north Gay st. -	3	2	2	1
Bounds, William A., carpenter, res e Burgess st.	1	2		1
Bogardus & Co., dealers in general hardware, s w				
quarter Public Square.				
BOGARDUS, W. P., (of the above firm,) resi-				
dence n w cor Gay and Burgess street. - -	1	3		2
Bonar, William, farmer, res north Main street. -	1	2		
Bryant, G. M., livery & feed stable, near foot of				
Main street, res cor Gay and Pleasant sts. -	1	4		3
Bryant, Isaac G., " " " -	1			
BRYANT, O. F., cooper, east Front, residence				
west Gambier street. - - - - - -	2	2	1	1

8

PRESIDENTIAL TICKETS.

——— o ———

DEMOCRATIC.
FOR PRESIDENT,
SAMUEL J. TILDEN, *of New York.*
FOR VICE PRESIDENT,
THOMAS A. HENDRICKS, *of Indiana.*

PRESIDENTIAL ELECTORS AT LARGE,
GRANVILLE W. STOKES, *of Warren County,*
WILLIAM LANG, *of Seneca* "

ELECTOR, 9TH DISTRICT,
FRENCH W. THORNHILL, *of Union County.*

———————

REPUBLICAN.
FOR PRESIDENT,
RUTHERFORD B. HAYES, *of Ohio.*
FOR VICE PRESIDENT,
WILLIAM A. WHEELER, *of New York.*

PRESIDENTIAL ELECTORS AT LARGE,
AARON F. PERRY, *of Hamilton County.*
EDWARD H. BOHM, *of Cuyahoga* "

ELECTOR, 9TH DISTRICT,
JOHN J. HANE, *of Marion County.*

———————

PROHIBITION.
FOR PRESIDENT,
GREEN CLAY SMITH, *of Kentucky.*
FOR VICE PRESIDENT,
GIDEON T. STEWART, *of Ohio.*

PRESIDENTIAL ELECTORS AT LARGE,
LEWIS BARNES, *of Delaware County,*
JAMES M. COULTER, *of Franklin* "

ELECTOR, 9TH DISTRICT.
THOMAS EVANS, JR., *of Delaware County.*

———————

INDEPENDENT (GREENBACK)
FOR PRESIDENT,
PETER COOPER, *of New York.*

FOR VICE PRESIDENT,
SAMUEL F. CARY, *of Ohio.*

The Mt. Vernon M. and N-Board Agency does not belong to the Insurance Board Organization.	Popu-lation.		Minors.	
	M	F	M	F
Bryant, C. E., physician, cor Main and Chestnut, residence near Columbus road.				
Bryant, Samuel, farmer, res near Columbus road.				
Bumpus, Mrs. Mary, res cor High & Mulberry. -	2	2	2	1
Bumpus, Sarah L., " " " -		1		
Bumpus, Fred., assessor 2d ward, res w Gambier.	1	2		1
Bumpus, Salathiel, cooper, " " -	3	2	2	1
Bumpus, H. A., grocer, Sandusky st.,res Sandusky	1	3		2
Boorn, Albert H., blacksmith, res " -	1	1		
Bridge, Emma P., brds with H. B. Curtis, "Round Hill." - - - - - - - - -		1		
Briggs, E. H., pattern maker, res Sandusky st. -	1	3		
Britt, James, moulder, res Sandusky street. -	3	2	2	
Blythe, Robert, stone cutter, res e Elizabeth st. -	2	2	1	
BOPE, CHARLES A., dealer in hardware, iron, nails, &c. Also, dealer in lump and nut coal, Weaver's old stand, s Main, res n Main st. -	2	2	1	
BOWLAND, ROBERT M., dealer in boots and shoes s e cor Main & Vine, res Mansfield ave.	2	1	1	
Barber, A., farmer, res Pleasant township.				
Bartlett, John, farmer, res north Main street. -	2	1	1	
Bartlett, Thomas, tinner, s Main, res e Gambier.	3	2	2	1
Bartlett, A. A., " n e cor Main and Front, residence west Gambier street. - - -	1	3		2
Bartlett & Young, livery and sale stable, w Vine.				
Bartlett, T. M., (of the above firm,) res cor Vine and Mechanic streets. - - - - -	2	1	1	
Branagan, Patrick, peddler, res west High street.	7	3	6	2
Blanchard, Mrs. Delia, residence " " " -	1	2	1	1
Blanchard, Fannie, teacher, " " " "				
Blanchard, Mrs. Augusta, res Front & McKenzie.		1		
BIRD, WILLIAM, (of the firm of Byers & B.,) dealer in hardware, stoves, &c., south Main, residence west High street. - - - -	2	4	1	3
Baird, J. Burr, cabinet maker, res w High street.	3	1	2	
Baird, Obediah, shoemaker, res north West st. -	1			
Baird, Oliver, cabinet maker, res " " " -	2	2	1	1
Baird, Mrs. Cornelia, dress maker, res Sperry's block, Public Square. - - - - -	2	1	2	
Benoy, Mrs. Jane, res cor Chester & Washington.	2	2	2	1
Benoy, Franklin, boiler maker, res " -	1			
Benoy, Charles, machinist, res " -	1			
Barrabell, Mrs. Mary, res Monroe street. - -		2		
Barrabell, John, res " " -	1			
Bloom, Mrs. Catharine, res west Burgess street. -		2		1
Benson, Mrs. ——, res Prospect street. - -		6		4
Burriss, William, blacksmith, res Sandusky st. -	1	1		
Bowden, John, machinist, " " " -	1	2		1

DEMOCRATIC, REPUBLICAN AND PROHIBITION STATE AND COUNTY TICKETS.

DEMOCRATIC.

—o—

STATE TICKET.

For Secretary of State,
WILLIAM BELL.

For Supreme Judge,
WILLIAM E. FINK.

For Board of Public Works,
H. P. CLOUGH.

—o—

DISTRICT.

For Common Pleas Judges,
JOHN ADAMS,
SAMUEL M. HUNTER.

For Congress, 9th District,
E. F. POPPLETON.

—o—

COUNTY.

For Prosecuting Attorney,
CLARK IRVINE.

For Sheriff,
JOHN F. GAY.

For Commissioner,
JOHN PONTING.

For Infirmary Director,
R. H. BEBOUT.

For Coroner,
GEORGE SHIRA, M. D.

REPUBLICAN.

—o—

STATE TICKET.

For Secretary of State,
MILTON BARNES.

For Supreme Judge,
W. W. BOYNTON.

For Board of Public Works,
JAMES C. EVANS.

—o—

DISTRICT.

For Congress,
JOHN S. JONES.

For Common Pleas Judges,
JEROME BUCKINGHAM,
JOHN D. VANDEMAN.

—o—

COUNTY.

For Prosecuting Attorney,
J. B. GRAHAM.

For Sheriff,
CALVIN MAGERS.

For Commissioner,
T. R. HEAD.

For Infirmary Director,
ABRAHAM D. MELICK.

For Coroner,
S. C. THOMPSON, M. D.

Insure Yourselves and Property with *J. J. Fultz.*	Popula-tion.		M inors.	
	M	F	M	F
Bentz, Jacob, teamster, residence Madison street.	2	3	1	2
Bingham, R. B., carpenter, res n Mulberry " -	3	2	2	1
Branyan, J. H., blacksmith, cor Front & Gay sts. residence Catharine street. - - -	4	2	3	1
Branyan, Jessie F., res Catharine street.				
Buckland, Henry, teamster, res south Main st. -	1			
Buckland, Mrs. Henry, boarding house, s Main.		4		
Buckland, Anson, boards with Mrs. Buckland. -	1			
Bond, Mrs. Sarah J., res east Front street. -		2		
Beatty, John, res east Front street. - -	1	2		
Bascom, ——, carriage maker, bds Mrs Buckland's	1			
Brooks, Josephine, residence east Vine street. -		1		
Brooks, James, works Gas house, res w Front st.	1	1		
Burrows, E. B., pastor Congregational church, residence east Gambier street. - - -	1	2		
Bryan, Martha, help at Bergin House. - - -		1		
Brauneck, Edward, porter at Rowley House. -	1			
Berry, Clement, [c] laborer, res w Gambier st. -	1			
Brentlinger, G. W., carpenter, res cor Mulberry and Gambier streets. - - - -	1			
Breece, Stanley, stone mason, res w Gambier st. -	4	1	3	
Ball, Judson, farmer, res Chesterville road.				
Ball, Andrew, " " "				
Ball, Aaron, " " "				
BALL, FREDERICK M., cooper, w Gambier street, residence Martinsburgh road.				
BALL, DALLAS, cooper, west Gambier street, residence Clinton township.				
Braggins, Edward, painter, res w Vine street. -	2	2	1	1
Burney, Daniel, laborer, res south Harrison st. -	2	2	1	1
BANK—Knox County Savings, north Main, between Public Square and Chestnut st.				
" —Knox County National, s e cor Main st. and Public Square.				
" —First National, n e cor Main & Vine sts.				
BRITTON, LEWIS, county treasurer, residence Howard township.				
Baugh, C. C., travelling agent, res n e cor Vine & Catharine streets. - - - -	2	2	1	1
Bushfield, John O., grocer, Public Square, residence Wooster avenue. - - - -	1	2		1

C

CURTIS, HENRY B., president Knox County National Bank, residence " Round Hill." -	1	3		
Curtis, L. B., ins. agent, res Cemetery avenue. -	2	4	1	3

PROHIBITION—STATE.

For Secretary of State,
E. S. CHAPMAN.

For Judge of Supreme Court,
D. W. GAGE.

For Board Public Works,
FERDI'D. SCHUMACHER.

For Congress—9th District,
LEVI L. BENSON, M. D.

PROHIBITION—COUNTY.

For Prosecuting Attorney,
H. CLAY ROBINSON.

For Sheriff,
TOWN'D. F. VAN VORIES.

For Commissioner,
URIAH WALKER.

For Infirmary Director,
ROLLIN F. BEACH.

For Coroner,
ABNER B. SHUMAN.

Non-Board and Mutual Companies a Specialty.   *J. J. Fultz.*

	Popula- tion.		Minors.	
	M	F	M	F
CURTIS, HENRY L., attorney, cor Chestnut & Main streets, res cor Sugar and Gay streets. -	2	5	1	3
Curtis, R. C., clerk with Adler Bros., res e Sugar.	3	2	2	1
Curtis, Mrs. Mary, residence west Chestnut. -	1	3	1	2
Curtis, Mrs. C. C., " Mansfield avenue. -		1		
Curtis, Charles C., " west Burgess street.	1	1		
Curtis, Hellen, teacher, " Mansfield avenue. -		3		
Craig, D. M., carriage maker, res " "	5	3	1	2
Copeland, Thomas, huckster, res n Mulberry st. -	2	1	1	
C. & G. Cooper & Co., Stationary, Portable, and Steam Farm Engine Manufacturers, shop n e corner Sandusky and Sugar streets.				
COOPER, CHARLES, (of the above firm,) residence west Sugar street. - - - -	1	5		
Cooper, Charles F., (son of Charles C.) w Sugar. -	1			
Cooper, Adele, residence west Sugar street.				
Cooper, Cora, " " "				
Cooper, Charles G., (of the firm of C. & G. C. & Co.) residence east Gambier street. - -	1	1		
Cooper Manufacturing Co., office foot of Main st.				
COOPER, JOHN, (of the above Co.) residence " Thistle Ridge."	1	1		
Cooper, Hugh Newton, res Thistle Ridge. -	1			
Cooper, Henry, policeman, res Wooster avenue. -	1	2		1
Cooper, Dan C., (of the firm of Irvine & Cooper,) restaurant, near foot of Main street, residence corner Main & Pleasant streets. -	2	2	1	
Cooper, Elias, tinner, res east Gambier street. -	1			
Cooper, Mrs. Thompson, res e " "		1		
Cooper, Kate, " " " -		1		
COOPER, Col. WILLIAM C., attorney, office south Main street, brds at James Sapp's, s Gay	1	3		1
Clucas, H., machinist, brds with D. Morris, west Chestnut street.	1			
Coventry, H., machinist, brds Central House. -	1	1		
Carr, J. L., clerk with W. T. Patton, brds with James Sapp, south Gay street. - -	1			
Calkins, Mrs. Susan, brds with Mrs. Rush, e High.		1		
Couch, Susie, milliner, s Main. res w Vine street.		1		
Cochran, David, carpenter, Harrison & Chestnut.	1	2		
Cochran, Cyphrain, planing mill, res w " -	1	1		
Cochran, Matthew, farmer, res w High street. -	1	1		
Cochran, John, laborer, res Coshocton avenue. -	2	1	1	
Cochran, Charles F., shoemaker, west High, residence north West street. - - - -	2	3	1	2
Cochran, Leroy, plasterer, res cor Oak & Rogers.	1	2		1
Cochran, William, " " east Gambier st.	2	2	1	1
Cochran, Joseph R., brick mason. " " -	1			

Established   1866.

JOHN S. BRADDOCK,

DEALER IN

Land Warrants, Scrip,

—AND—

ALL KINDS OF REAL ESTATE,

MOUNT VERNON, OHIO.

——o——

OFFICE—One Door East of First National Bank.   RESIDENCE, No. 189 West High Street.

REFERS BY PERMISSION TO
(Cashier FIRST NATIONAL BANK.
 "   KNOX CO. NAT. BANK.
("   KNOX CO. SAVINGS BANK.

LIVE STOCK STATISTICS—KNOX COUNTY—1875.

Horses,	 9,886	Wool shorn, . . 772,408 lbs.
" value,	. $501,046	No. of Dogs, . . 1919
Cattle,	. . . 18,096	No. of Sheep killed by Dogs,573
" value,	. $228,148	Value of Sheep killed, $1,757
Hogs,	. . . 21,422	Sheep injured by Dogs, 350
" value, .	. $75,945	Val. Sheep injur'd by dogs, $822
Sheep,	. . . 143,083	Total val. killed & inj'd. $2,579
" value,	. $251,396	

——◆——

ONE evening, during performances on the Organ of the Catholic Cathedral in Boston, a mouse, evidently drawn from his retreat by the mellow sounds, ran in front of the white linen which hangs on the inside of the sanctuary railing. Slowly sitting back on his haunches, he remained motionless as a statue, seemingly conscious of nothing except the rich, soft tones. Suddenly the organist made a change, and sharp, quick notes succeeded the gentle ones, and the little listener, with frightened air, quickly scampered away.

Insurance against loss from Fire and Lightning, by the Mt. Vernon M. & N-B. Insurance Agency.	Population.		Minors.	
	M	F	M	F
Cotton, E. W., attorney and surveyor, res e Front.	2	2	1	
Cotton, Rose E., residence east Front street.				
Cotton, T. B., blacksmith, boards Bergin House.	2	1	1	
Cotton & Rose, restaurant, n w cor Main & Front.				
COTTON, H. K., (of the above firm,) residence south Gay street. - - - - - -	1	1		
Cotton, Mrs. L. L., res Lybrand block, e Front.	3	1	3	
Cotton, Clinton, telegraph messenger, res "				
Carpenter, Perry, laborer, res east Gambier street.	1			
Carpenter, Mrs. ——, " " " " .		3		2
Carpenter, A., physician, s Main, res w High st.	2	3	1	
Carpenter, Belle, music teacher, " "				
CARPENTER, A. R., (of Graff & C.) produce dealer, foot Main street, res Mansfield avenue.	2	3	1	2
Cavanaugh, Michael, boiler maker, res w Chestnut	1			
Caswell, Mrs. Mary, res cor Mechanic & Chestnut		1		
Chancey, Mrs. Anne E., res west High street. -		2		1
Coates, Mrs. Maria, res corner Vine & Adams sts.		1		
Cole, Isaac, blacksmith, res north Norton street. -	1	1		
Cole, Silas " " south West " -	2	3	1	2
Cole, James, cabinet maker, res w Gambier st. -	2	1	1	
Cole, Frederick, C. Mt. V. & C. R.R., res e Vine.	1	1		
Coleman, Charles O., law student, res e Gambier.	1	1		
Coleman, Alexander, carpenter, res n Norton st. -	4	2	3	1
CORCORAN, DENNIS, grocer, west Vine, near Woodward block, res cor Vine & Mechanic sts	1	4		3
Council Chamber, e side n Gay street.				
County Commissioners' office, s side Chestnut btw Gay and McKenzie streets.				
County Surveyor's office, s side Chestnut btw Gay and McKenzie streets.				
County Jail, s side Chestnut btw Gay & McKenzie				
Court House, n side High btw Gay & McKenzie.				
Catholic Church, n e cor High & McKenzie sts.				
Catholic Parsonage, s e cor McKenzie & Chestnut				
Catholic Parochial School, n e cor " " High sts.				
Connelly, John, res cor High and Mulberry sts. -	1			
Connelly, Angeline, dress maker, res corner High and Mulberry streets. - - - - -		1		
Cullison, N. W., boarding house, w High street.	1	5		
Cullison, Alice, residence w High street.				
Cullison, Jennie, " " "				
Cullison, Minnie, " " "				
Condon, Philip, carpenter, res Sugar & Sandusky.	2	1	1	
Condon, Geo. W., " " " "	6	3	5	2
Crowell, F. S., photographer, cor Main and Vine, residence east Front street. - - - -		2	1	1
Clark, Thomas, painter, res east Vine street. -	3	2	2	1

9

OHIO--1803.

—— [o] ——

THE First General Assembly, of Ohio, under a State constitution, met at Chillicothe, March 1st, 1803.

Free White Males Over 21 Years of Age:

Adams county,	 906	Montgomery,	 526
Trumbull, .	 1111	Columbiana,	 542
Belmont,	 1030	Ross,	 1982
Butler,	 835	Clermont,	 755
Galia, .	 307	Scioto,	 249
Hamilton,	 1700	Franklin,	 240
Warren.	 854	Fairfield, .	 1051

Total population in 1803, ... 12,088

FIRST STATE OFFICERS:

Governor—Edwin Tiffin, of Hamilton county.
Secretary of State—William Creighton, Jr.
Auditor of State—Col. Thomas Gibson.
Treasurer of State—William McFarland.
Judges Supreme Court—R. J. Meigs, Jr., Samuel Huntington, William Sprigg.
Judges District Court—Francis Dunlavy, Wyllys Silliman, Calvin Pease.
Speaker of the Senate—Nathaniel Massie.
Speaker of the House—Michael Baldwin.

1876.
PRESENT STATE OFFICERS:

Governor—Rutherford B. Hayes, of Sandusky county.
Lieutenant-Governor—Thomas L. Young.
Speaker of the House—Charles H. Grosvenor.
Secretary of State—William Bell, Jr.
Auditor of State—James Williams.
Treasurer of State—Leroy M. Welsh.
Comptroller of the Treasury—William T. Wilson.
Attorney General—John Little.
Commissioner of Common Schools—Charles S. Smart.
Judges of Supreme Court—George Rex, John Welch, William White, William J. Gilmore, George W. McIlvaine.
Clerk Supreme Court—Arnold Green.
Board of Public Works—Peter Thatcher, Philip V. Herzing, Martin Schilder.
Commissioner of Railroads and Telegraphs—L. G. Delano.
State Librarian—Hiram H. Robinson.

	Popula- tion.		Minors	
You can get Cash or Mutual Fire Insurance with J. J. Fultz, Agt.	M	F	M	F
Clark, Fanny, residence south Gay street. - -		1		
Clark, Samuel W., saddler and harness maker, w Vine, residence e Chestnut street. - -	1	2	1	
Clark, T. L., lessee Kokosing Iron Works, foot of Main street, residence e Gambier street. -	1	3 ·		2
Clark, Mary, " " " •				
Clark, Jessie, " " "				
Clark, T. Eugene, physician, res e Gambier st. -	1			
Clark, John, draughtsman, at Kokosing Iron Works, res cor Front and Gay streets. -	2	4	1	3
Clark, F. G., Paymaster C. Mt. V. & C. Railroad, boards at Bergin House. - - -	1	.		
Clark, Robert, clerk, res cor Main and Sugar sts.	2	4	1	2
Clark, Joseph, laborer, res Coshocton avenue. -	2	3	1	2
CASSIL, ALEXANDER, county auditor, resi- dence east High street. - - - -	4	1	3	
Cassil & Chase, dealers in books, music, station- ery, &c., south Main street.				
Cassil, Austin A., (of the above firm,) res e High.	1			
Cassil, Wm. R., clerk auditor's office, res e " -				
Cassel, B. S., farmer, res Chesterville road.				
Chapman, Stephen, carpenter, res w Sugar street.	1	2		1
Chapman, Jennie, residence " "				
Chapman, Joseph, engr. C. Mt. V. & C. R.R., res- idence east Vine street. - - - -	1	2		1
Chapman, Charles, fireman, C. Mt. V. & C. R.R., residence east Vine street. - - -	1			
Chapin, C. H., clerk, residence north Gay street.	2	1	1	
Charlton, Henry, brick mason, residence corner Gay & Elizabeth streets. - - - -	1	2		1
Claypool, Millard, painter, res e Gambier street. -	1			
Clayton, Joseph, carpenter, res e Burgess street. -	3	2	2	1
Clayton, Charles, blacksmith, res w Front street.	1		1	
Coyle, L. D., plasterer, res n Gay street. - -	1	2		1
Carey, Waldo, medical student, res n Main street.	1			
Curran, Thomas, boiler maker, res Sandusky st.	4	8	3	7
Curran, Sarah, " "				
Curran, Elizabeth, " "				
Craft, W. E., carpenter, res e Chestnut street. -	3	2	2	
Craft, Eugene, medical student, e " " -	1			
Craft, George, painter, res e Hamtramck street. -	3	3	2	2
Chase, D. W., (of the firm of Chase & Cassil,) res- idence Cincinnati, Ohio. •				
Chase, E. J., (of the firm of Chase & Dawson, Eagle mills, w Gambier st.,) res Granville road.				
Church, Mrs. C. B., residence e Front street. -		2		1
Church, Philip, " " - -	1			
Church, Brook, stone mason, " - -	1	1		

KNOX COUNTY FORMED, MARCH 1, 1808.

Population of Knox, 1870, 26,333.

In 1808, Knox county cast 83 votes for Samuel Huntington, and 4 votes for Thomas Kirker, for Governor: the candidates that year were Samuel Huntington, Thomas Worthington and Thomas Kirker.

KNOX COUNTY VOTE ON GOVERNOR.

1810—For R. J. Meigs, Jr., 99, T. Worthington, 90.

1812— " R. J. Meigs, Jr., 113.

1814— " T. Worthington, 383.

1816— " T. Worthington, 447, Dunlap, 2, Brown, 23.

1818— " Brown, 532, Dunlap, 38.

1820— " Brown, 675, Morrow, 24, W. H. Harrison, 2.

1822— " Morrow, 30, Trimble, 80, W. W. Irwin, 905.

1824— " Morrow, 716, Trimble, 582.

1826— " Trimble, 1729, Bigger, 19, Campbell, 15, Tappan, 22.

1828— " Trimble, 776, John W. Campbell, 1352.

1830— " McArthur, 1093, Robert Lucas, 993.

1832— " Robert Lucas, 1783, David Lyman, 948.

1834— " Robert Lucas, 1802, James Findlay, 1103.

1836— " Eli Baldwin, 1829, Joseph Vance, 1398.

1838— " Wilson Shannon, 2645, Joseph Vance, 1922.

1840— " Wilson Shannon, 2936, Thomas Corwin, 2470.

1842— " Wilson Shannon, 2936, T. Corwin, 2194, King, 125.

1844— " D. Tod, 3289, M. Bartley, 2696, King, 150.

1846— " D. Tod, 2647, W. Bebb, 2103, Samuel Lewis, 190.

1848— " J. B. Weller, 3224, S. Ford, 2288, Scattering, 32.

1850— " R. Wood, 2700, W. Johnson, 1909, E. Smith, 267.

1851— " R. Wood, 2454, S. F. Vinton, 1533, S. Lewis, 409.

1853— " W. Medill, 2159, N. Barrere, 869, S. Lewis, 1068.

1855— " W. Medill, 1916, A. Trimble, 219, Chase, 2166.

1857— " Chase, 2385, H. B. Payne, 2223, P. Van Trump, 82.

1859— " W. Dennison, 2603, R. P. Ranney, 2583.

1861— " D. Tod, 2831, H. J. Jewett, 1998.

1863— " J. Brough, 3160, C. L. Vallandingham, 2552.

1865— " J. D. Cox, 2629, George W. Morgan, 2428.

1867— " R. B. Hayes, 2814, A. G. Thurman, 2811.

1869— " G. H. Pendleton, 2798, R. B. Hayes, 2761.

1871— " G. W. McCook, 2820, Noyes, 2767, Stewart, 13.

1873— " Allen, 2762, Noyes, 2108, Stewart, 432, Collins, 35.

1875— " W. Allen, 3132, Hayes, 2885, Odell, 101.

Insure in the Companies represen *by* **J. J. Fultz, Agt.**	Popula-tion.		Minors.	
	M	F	M	F
Crouse, George, residence e Gambier street. - -	1	1		
Christian Church, s side e Vine, between Gay and McKenzie streets.				
Central House, (J. C. Lee,) n w side Pub. Sqr.				
Cook, John, tailor, boards at Mrs. Buckland's. -	1			
Campbell, Mrs. Ann, res Gambier Hill.				
Campbell, Elizabeth, " "				
CAMPBELL, HARRY, farmer, res Gambier Hill.				
Campbell, William, [c] help at Bergin House. -	1			
Cresap, Miss Gerrie, seamstress, res Israel's block, north Main street. - - - - -		1		
Crisp, Thomas, help at Bergin House. - -	1			
CROUCH, W. A., Photographer, Hill's block, n w cor Vine & Gambier, res same building.	3	2	2	1
Culbertson, Mrs. Narcissa, res n Gay street. -		1		
Culbertson, W. C., attorney, e High, res n Gay. -	1			
Cain, Thomas, laborer, res e Chestnut street. -	2	2	1	1
Cavin, Edward, dealer in organs, " " -	1	3		2
Carter, P. C., clerk, res cor Vine & Mechanic sts.	1			
Carter, William, laborer, res n Catharine street. -	4	3	3	2
Cameron, James, laborer, res e Sugar street. -	1			
Cassidy, Mrs. Bridget, res e Burgess street. - -		3		1
Cassidy, Mary, " " "				
Cassidy, Lizzie, " " "				
Crandall, Russell T., assessor 5th ward, residence e Hamtramck street. - -	2	2	1	
CRANDALL, P. B., clerk in Baldwin's Hat & Fur Store, res cor Mulberry & Lamartin sts. -	1	1		
Cummins, Mrs. Blair, res e Burgess street. - -		1		
Cummins, Marcus, carpenter, res e Burgess street.	3	2	2	1
Cummins, Frank, " " " " -	1			
Cummins, John, " " " " -	1			
Coe, W. H., brick and stone mason, res corner Gambier and Harrison streets. - - -	1	2		1
Cox, Harvey, farmer, res Fredericktown road.				
Conner, John, laborer, res w Vine street. - -	3	3	2	2
Conner, Peter, " res s Rogers street. -	2	3	1	
Connells, John, carriage painter, res corner Walnut and Gambier streets. - - - -	1	1		
Chisholms, Samuel, blacksmith, res cor Mulberry and Gambier streets. - - - -	1	2		1
Christie, William, laborer, res w Front street. -	3	1	2	
Christie, James, " " " -	1			
Chambers, Benjamin, farmer, res Newark road.				
Carnahan, Nancy, help at Bergin House. - -		1		
CASE, AARON, dealer in tobacco, cigars, pipes, &c., store and residence s Main street. - -		3		2

KNOX COUNTY.
—— [o] ——

Lt. Governor—ROBERT C. KIRK, of Knox County, 1860.

MEMBERS CONSTITUTIONAL CONVENTIONS.

2d *Convention*, 1850—Matthew H. Mitchell, John Sellers.
3d   "   1873—Richard S. Tulloss.

STATE SENATORS.

1808—Knox, Fairfield & Licking—Elnathan Scofield.
1809—Same counties—Jacob Burton, Elnathan Scofield.
1810-11—Same counties—Wm. Trimble, Rbt. F. Slaughter.
1812-13—Knox and Licking—William Gavit.
1814—Knox, Licking and Richland—William Gass.
1815—Same counties—William Gavit.
1816-17—Same counties—Mordecai Bartley.
1818-19—Same counties—John Spencer.
1820—Knox and Richland—William Gass.
1821-2—Same counties—John Shaw.
1823-4—Same counties—William Gass.
1825-6—Same counties—Daniel S. Norton.
1827-8—Same counties—William Gass.
1829-30—Same counties—Thomas Rigdon.
1831—Same counties—William Gass.
1832-3—Knox and Coshocton—Byram Leonard.
1834-5—Same counties—James Ravenscroft.
1836-7—Knox, Coshocton and Holmes—Peres Sprague.
1838-9—Same counties—James Matthews.
1840-1—Knox and Coshocton—Byram Leonard.
1842-3—Same counties—John Johnston.
1844-5—Knox and Holmes—Jacob B. Koch.
1846—Same counties—Nicholas Spindler.
1847—Knox county—Nicholas Spindler.
1848-9—Knox and Holmes—Asa G. Dimmock.
1850—Same counties—Lawrence Van Buskirk.
1852—Knox and Morrow—Lawrence Van Buskirk.
1854—Same counties—John T. Creigh.
1856—Same counties—Robert C. Kirk.
1858—Same counties—Davis Miles.
1860—Same counties—William Bonar.
1862—Knox, Morrow, Holmes and Wayne—Davis Miles.
1864—Same counties—Joseph C. Devin.

Insure Yourselves in the C. M. L. & H. I. Co., of Mt. Vernon, O.	Popu-lation.		Minors.	
	M	F	M	F
Case, Mrs. Aaron, dress maker, e Vine st., opposite Post Office, res s Main street.				
Clements, John W., sash factory, n Sandusky st. residence corner Gambier and Mechanic sts.	1	2		1
Creighton, Mrs. Rosanna, res s Mulberry st. -		1		
Crowl, John, residence Railroad street. - -	1	1		
Critchfield & Graham, attorneys, Kirk Hall.				
CRITCHFIELD, J. D., (of the above firm,) brds at Bergin House. - - - - - -	1			
Critchfield, William, res w Sugar street. - -	2	1	1	
CRITCHFIELD, C. E., attorney, s Main, over Armstrong & Tilton's store, res e Chestnut st.	2	2	1	1
Conklin, William, miller, res n Norton street. -	2	2	1	1
Conklin, Edward, laborer, res Madison street. -	2	1	1	
Colville, Thomas, farmer, res Pleasant township.				
Colville, Milton, " " "				
Canning, William, miller, res n Norton street.	3	2	2	1
Caraghan, Dennis, laborer, " " "	1	1		
Caraghan, Michael, machinist, " "	1			
Cunningham, Charles, carpenter, res Madison st.	1			
Cunningham, Mrs. Sarah, res Madison street. -		1		
Crevling, Samuel, farmer, res Martinsburgh road.				
Crevling, Charles, " " "				

D

	M	F	M	F
DAVIS, JOSEPH S., ex-Probate Judge, and Sec'y. C. Mt. V. & C. R.R., res n Mulberry st.	1	2		
Davis, Mary, residence "				
Davis, Rollin H., jeweler, residence "	1			
Davis, Capt. Henry, U. S. A., " "	1			
Davis, F. A., clerk C. Mt. V. & C. R.R., residence north Main street. - - - - - -	2	1	1	
Davis, John C., tailor, residence w Burgess street.	1	4		2
Davis, Mary L., " " "				
Davis, Frank M., " " "	1			
Davis, James B., [c] laborer, res e High "	1	3		2
DAVIS, SAMUEL, Sr., township trustee, residence Columbus road.				
Davis, Samuel, Jr., clerk at Rowley House. - -	1			
Davis, Elizabeth, sales lady with W. C. Sapp, residence Columbus road.				
Davis, J. R., laborer, residence s Main street. -	3		2	
Darcy, Francis J., clerk, res cor Vine & Mulberry.	1		1	
Durbin, Thomas, banker, s Main, res e Gambier.	1	2		
Durbin, Leander, laborer, res s Catharine street.	2	1	1	
Daubert, J. T., huckster, w Vine, res e Front st. -	1	2		1

1866—Knox, Morrow, Holmes & Wayne—F. H. Hurd, L. R.
　　　Critchfield.
1868—Same counties—George Rex, C. H. Scribner.
1870—Same counties—Hinchman H. Prophet.
1872—Same counties—Henry D. McDowell.
1874—Same counties—Daniel Paul.
1876—Same counties—John Ault.

HOUSE OF REPRESENTATIVES.

1808—Knox and Licking—Alexander Holden.
1809—Same counties—William Gass.
1810—Same counties—Jeremiah R. Munson.
1811—Same counties—William Gass.
1812—Knox—Samuel Kratzer.
1813—Knox and Richland—William Gass.
1814—Knox—Samuel Kratzer.
1815—Knox and Richland—Alexander Enos.

KNOX COUNTY.

1816-17—Jonathan Miller.
1818—William W. Farquhar.
1819-20-1—Royal D. Simmons.
1822—Hosmer Curtis.
1823—Royal D. Simmons.
1824—Thomas Rigdon.
1825—John Shaw.
1826—William Robson.
1827—Thomas Rigdon.
1828—C. Colerick, B. Leonard.
1829—Byram Leonard.
1830—John Greer.
1831—Charles Colerick.
1832-3—John Schooler.
1834-5—Peres Sprague.
1836—S. W. Hildreth, M. Tracy.
1837—Marvin Tracy.
1838—James Elliott.
1839—Byram Leonard.
1840—N. Spindler, Dr McGugin.
1841—Caleb J. McNulty.
1842—C J McNulty, N. Spindler

1843—William Smith.
1844—J. McFarland, G. Ankeny
1845—William H. Smith.
1846—J M'Farland, E W Cotton
1847—Emmit W. Cotton.

KNOX AND HOLMES.

1848—J Vorhes, L Van Buskirk
1849—Wm. Given, E. Boggs.
1850—E. Glasgo, S. F. Gilerist.

KNOX.

1852—James Withrow.
1854—Jacob Merrin.
1856—G. W. True, B. F. Smith.
1858—W. McCreary, W. B. Cox
1860—William B. Cox.
1862—Wait Whitney.
1864—Columbus Delano.
1866—Henry B. Banning.
1868—Robert Moffet.
1870—John D. Thompson.
1872—William C. Cooper.
1874—Allen J. Beach.
1876—Abel Hart, Jr.

Insure in the Companies represented _by_ _J. J. Fultz, Agt._	Popu-lation.		Minors	
	M	F	M	F
Daugherty, Frank, brakeman C. Mt. V. & C. RR., residence e Front street. - - - -	1	1		
Dettra & Sanderson, livery & sale stable, w Front				
Dettra, John P., (of the above firm,) res e Front.	2	2	1	1
Durr, David, cabinet maker, bds Mrs. Buckland's	1			
DELANO, COLUMBUS, Pres't. 1st Nat. Bank, residence Martinsburgh road.				
Delano, John S., farmer, res Martinsburgh road.				
Devoe, Joel, carpenter, res Gambier road.				
Devoe, Almeda, teacher, " "				
Devoe, Elsadia, res " "				
Devoe, Mary, teacher, res e Chestnut street. -		1		
Devin & Curtis, [H. L. Curtis,] attorneys, n e cor Main and Chestnut streets.				
DEVIN, JOSEPH C., (of the above firm,) residence n w cor Main & Chestnut streets. - -	2	4	1	1
Devin, Bessie H., res n w cor Main & Chestnut.				
Dickey, James, residence w High street. - -	1	2		
Dickey, Joseph F., " " " -	1			
DUNBAR, W. B., deputy county treasurer, residence n Gay street. - - - - - -	2	1	1	
Dunbar & Lennon, attorneys, Miller block, s Main				
Dunbar, William, (of the above firm,) res e High	1	1		
Dunbar, Hattie, teacher, res e High street. - -		1		
Dunbar, Callie, " " " -		1		
Davidson, Mrs. A. E., boarding house, e High st.	1	4	1	
Davidson, Truman, omnibus driver, res e " -	1			
Davidson, Mrs. Ellen, residence s Mulberry st. -		1		
Davidson, Ella, dress maker, res s " -		1		
Dunham, J. S., clerk with Chase & Cassil, res e High	1	1		
DUNHAM, WILLIAM E., ex-County Treasurer, residence Wayne township.				
Dunham, Frederick, farmer, res Clinton township				
Dunham, Jacob, farmer, " " "				
Downs, Worth S., painter, brds Central House. -	1	1		
Denny, V., boarding house, south Mulberry st. -	4	3	3	2
DENNY, JOHN, Commercial Traveler, New York House, residence south Gay street. -	3	3	2	1
Dennis, Allen, residence east Chestnut street. -	1			
Doty, Robert, tailor, residence east Vine street. -	2	3	1	
Doty, Charles W., medical student, res e Vine st.				
Doty, William, residence east Vine street. - -	1			
Doty, Thomas, " " " " - -	1			
Doty, Clifton, machinist, res cor Monroe & Chester	1			
Doty, Mrs. Lydia, " " " -	1	3	1	2
Doty, Samuel, painter, residence w Vine street. -	2	2	1	1
Doyle, James, night watchman, Kokosing Iron Works, residence south Mechanic street. -	1	2		1

10

Signers of Declaration of Independence.

NAMES.	REP'S'D.	BORN.	DIED.	AGE
Adams, John,	Mass	Oct 30, 1735	July 4, 1826	92
Adams, Samuel,	Mass	Sept 22, 1732	Oct 2, 1803	82
Bartlett, Joseph,	N H	Nov — 1729	May 19, 1795	66
Braxton, Carter,	Va	Sept 10, 1736	Oct 10, 1797	61
Carroll, Charles,	Md	Sept 20, 1737	Nov 14, 1832	96
Chase, Samuel,	Md	Apr 17, 1741	June 19,1811	70
Clark, Abraham,	N J	Feb 15, 1741	Sept —, 1794	69
Clymer, George,	Pa	— —, 1739	Jan 24, 1813	74
Ellery, William,	R I	Dec 22, 1727	Feb 15, 1820	73
Floyd, William,	N Y	Dec 17, 1734	Aug 4, 1821	87
Franklin, Benjamin,	Pa	Jan 17, 1706	Apr 17, 1790	84
Gerry, Elbridge,	Mass	July 17, 1744	Nov 23, 1814	70
Gwinnett, Button,	Ga	— —, 1732	May 27, 1779	47
Hall, Lyman,	Ga	— —, 1721	Feb —, 1784	63
Hancock, John,	Mass	— —, 1737	Oct 8, 1793	55
Harrison, Benjamin,	Va	— —, —	— —, 1791	—
Hart, John,	N J	— —, 1715	— —, 1780	65
Heyward, T. Jr.,	S C	— —, 1746	Mar —, 1809	63
Hewes, Joseph,	N C	— —, 1730	Nov 19, 1779	49
Hooper, William,	N C	June 17,1742	Oct —, 1790	48
Hopkins, Stephen,	R I	Mar 7, 1707	July 13, 1785	78
Hopkinson, Francis,	N J	— —, 1737	May 9, 1791	53
Huntington, Sam'l.,	Ct	July 2, 1732	Jan 5, 1796	64
Jefferson, Thomas,	Va	Apr 13, 1743	July 4, 1826	83
Lee, Francis L.,	Va	Oct 14, 1734	Apr —, 1797	63
Lee, Rich'd. Henry,	Va	Jan 20, 1732	June 19,1794	62
Lewis, Francis,	N Y	Mar —, 1713	Dec 30, 1803	90
Livingston, Philip,	N Y	Jan 15, 1716	June 12,1778	62
Lynch, Thomas, Jr.,	S C	Aug 5, 1749	at sea, 1790	41
McKean, Thomas,	Del	Mar 19, 1734	June 24,1817	84
Middleton, Arthur,	S C	— — 1743	Jan 1, 1788	45
Morris, Lewis,	N Y	— —, 1726	Jan 22, 1798	72
Morris, Robert,	Pa	— —, 1733	Mar 8, 1806	73
Morton, John,	Pa	— —, 1724	Apr —, 1777	54
Nelson, Thomas, Jr.,	Va	Dec 26, 1738	Jan 4, 1789	51
Paca, William,	Md	Oct 31, 1740	— —, 1799	60
Paine, Rob't. Treat,	Mass	— —, 1731	May 11, 1814	84
Penn, John,	N C	May 17, 1741	Oct 26, 1789	47
Read, George,	Del	— —, 1734	— —, 1798	64
Rodney, Cæsar,	Del	— —, 1730	— —, 1783	53
Ross, George,	Pa	— —, 1730	July —, 1780	50
Rush, Benj., M. D.	Pa	Dec 24, 1745	Apr 19, 1813	68
Rutledge, Edward,	S C	Nov —, 1735	Jan 23, 1800	65
Sherman, Roger,	Ct	Apr 19, 1721	July 23, 1793	73
Smith, James,	Pa	— —, 1720	July 11, 1806	86
Stockton, Richard,	N J	Oct 1, 1730	Feb 28, 1781	51
Stone, Thomas,	Md	— —, 1742	Oct 5, 1787	45
Taylor, George,	Pa	— —, 1716	Feb 23, 1781	65
Thornton, Matthew,	N H	— —, 1714	June 24,1803	89
Walton, George,	Ga	— —, 1740 ·	Feb 2, 1804	64
Whipple, William,	N H	— —, 1730	Nov 28, 1785	55
Williams, William,	Ct	Apr 18, 1731	Aug 2, 1811	81
Wilson, James,	Pa	— —, 1742	Aug 28, 1798	56
Witherspoon, John,	N J	Feb 5, 1726	Nov 10, 1794	72
Walcott, Oliver,	Ct	Nov 26, 1726	Dec 1, 1797	72
Wythe, George,	Va	— —, 1726	June 8, 1800	74

	Popu-lation.		Minors	
Insurance against loss from Fire and Lightning, by the Mt. Vernon M. & N-B. Insurance Agency.	M	F	M	F
DOYLE, JOHN M., machinist, residence south Mechanic street. - - - - -	2	3	1	2
Doyle, Edward, laborer, res Sandusky street. -	4	2	3	1
Daniels, O. G., insurance agent, Banning Hall, res east High street. - - - - -	3	3	2	1
Duncan, Samuel, laborer, res w Vine street. -	1			
Donnelly, Sarah, dress maker, cor High & Gay. -		3		
Dermody, Martin, tailor, res cor Mulberry and Burgess streets. - - - - -	2	3	1	2
Dermody, Mrs. Bridget, res s Mulberry street. -	2	5	2	4
Dawson, Joseph, (of the firm of Chase & D., Eagle Mills,) res w Vine street. - - -	2	1	1	
Derkins, John, tailor, res w Gambier street. - -	3	5	2	4
Derkins, James O., painter, res w " " -	1			
Disney, Rev. B. V., colporteur, res e Front st. -	1	2		1
Dixon, Sophia, res w Gambier street. - - -		1		
Dixon, Ellen, milliner & dress maker, e Vine, opposite post office, res w Gambier street. -		1		
Dixon, J. F., laborer, residence n Norton street. -	2	2	1	1
Day, Ermina, teacher, res n Mulberry street. -		2		
Dunlap, Mrs. Mary, residence Sandusky street. -		1		
Dypert, Jonas, laborer, " Railroad " -	2	2	1	1
Dry, Henry, laborer, B. & O. R.R., res Chester st.	3	1	2	
Dry, Paul, " " -	1	4		3
Dove, Emory, " res Calhoun street. -	1	1		
Delany, Patrick, laborer C. Mt. V. & C. R.R., residence w Sugar street. - - - -	1			
Delany, Mrs. Mary, res w Sugar street. - -		2		
DEMOCRATIC BANNER office, s w corner of Main & Gambier streets. L. Harper, editor.				

E

Elliott, John, traveling agent, res e Hamtramck.	2		1	
Elliott, Mrs. John, dress maker, s Mulberry, res e Hamtramck street. - - - -		1		
Elliott, Mrs. Catharine, res Mansfield avenue. -		2		
Elliott, Mrs. Martha, residence e High street. -		1		
Elliott, Elizabeth, " "		1		
Elliott, Mrs. Susanna, " cor High & West.		1		
Elliott, Richard, boiler maker, " " -	1			
Elliott, Armor B., photographer, " " -	1			
Elliott, J. B., farmer, res Monroe township.				
Ewalt, Isaac, " " Green Valley road.				
Ewalt, Henry, " " Delaware "				
EWALT, W. B., attorney, office Kirk Hall, res Delaware road.				

BAKER BROS,

DRUGGISTS,

MT. VERNON, O.

SIGN OF THE BIG

DEALERS IN

Paints, Oils, Dye Stuffs, Patent Medicines, Perfumery, Toilet Articles, and Druggists' Fancy Goods. Our Stock is from first-class, reliable dealers and manufacturers, and we challenge competition in price of goods, and comparison, as to quality, with any store of the kind.

Our Assortment of Reliable PATENT MEDICINES is complete.

WINES AND LIQUORS,

FOR MEDICINAL PURPOSES ONLY.

A very large and new assortment of Perfumery, Toilet and Fancy Articles, and Druggists' Sundries, including all such goods as are usually kept in a first-class Drugstore. Remember,

All Goods Warranted as Represented.

You can get Cash or Mutual Fire Insurance with J. J. Fultz. Agt.	Popu-lation.		Minors	
	M	F	M	F
Ewalt, Samuel, farmer, res McKinney road.				
EWALT, JOHN M., cashier Knox County National Bank, res e Vine street. - - -	2	3	1	1
Ewalt, Mrs. Eliza, boarding house, s w corner of Gambier and Gay streets. - - -	3	4	3	2
Ewing, D. & J. D., attorneys, J. W. Miller's block, south Main street.				
Ewing, David, (of the above firm,) res n Mulberry	1	1		
Ewing, John D., (of the above firm,) Justice of the Peace, s Main, res n Mulberry street. -	1			
Ewing, William, boiler maker, res w Chestnut st.	1			
Ewing, Harry, " " " n Norton st.	2	1	1	
Earnest, Mrs. Sarah, res cor Vine and Jefferson. -	1	4	1	3
Earnest, Vine, milliner, s Main, " "				
EARL, WILLIAM, gardener and trimmer, residence Columbus road.				
Errett & Banning, dealers in stoves, tinware, &c. south Main, near Gambier street.				
ERRETT, ISAAC, of the above firm, residence corner Vine and Mulberry streets. - - -	4	2	3	
Errett, Mrs. Mary W., res w Vine street. - -	2	2	2	1
Errett, Elizabeth, " " "				
Errett, William, " e Gambier street. -	1	3		2
Edwards, Ira, " n West "	1	1		
Ellis, J. Encell, clerk, brds with J. Sapp, s Gay st.	1			
Elder, Mrs. Julia, brds at Dr. Burr's, e High st. -		1		
Elder, Letitia S., teacher, brds at C. Peterman's. -		1		
Eggleston, Hiram, machinist, res w Sugar street.	2	2	1	1
EGGLESTON, E. R., physician, office and residence 156 east High street. - - -	2	2	1	1
Eggleston, Byron, physician, office and residence east Vine street. - - - -	3	2	2	1
ELWELL, W. T., deputy sheriff, residence e Gambier street. - - - - -	1	2		1
Evans, Mrs. Mary W., res s Mulberry street. -		3		
Evans, Anna, music teacher, " " -		1		
Evans, Job, residence " " -	1			
Evans, Thomas, farmer, res w Chestnut " -	1	1		
Evans, Mrs. Matilda, res s Mulberry "	1	1	1	
Express Company, [Union,]) United—office s side of				
Express Company, [United States,]) Public Square, W. J. Horner, agent.				
English, Mrs. Margaret, res Young & Raymond's block, Public Square. - - - -	1	1	1	

F

Fredrick, Thomas P., Sr., Mayor, res e Burgess.	2	1	1	

EMPHASIS.

SOME years ago there was a student at the Theological Seminary at Andover, who had an excellent opinion of his own talents. On one occasion he asked the professor who taught elocution at the time, " What do I specially need to learn in this department?" " You ought first to learn to read," said the professor. " Oh, I can read now," replied the student. The professor handed the young man a Testament, and pointing to the twenty-fifth verse of the twenty-fourth chapter of Luke's gospel, he asked him to read that. The student read, " Then he said unto them, O fools, and slow of heart *to believe* all the prophets have spoken." " Ah," said the professor, " they were fools for believing the prophets, were they?" Of course that was not right, and so the young man tried again. " O fools, and slow of heart to believe *all* that the prophets have spoken." " The prophets, then, were sometimes liars?" asked the professor. No: " O fools, and slow of heart to believe all that the *prophets* have spoken." " According to this reading," the professor suggested, " the prophets were notorious liars." This was not a satisfactory conclusion, and so another trial was made. "O, fools and slow of heart to believe all that the prophets have *spoken*." " I see now," said the professor, " the prophets wrote the truth, but they spoke lies." This last criticism discouraged the student, and he acknowledged that he did not know how to read. The difficulty lies in the fact that the words "slow of heart to believe" applies to the whole of the latter part of the sentence, and emphasis on any particular word entirely destroys the meaning.

| *Insure Yourselves in the C. M. L. &* | Popu-lation. | | Minors | |
H. I. Co., of Mt. Vernon, O.	M	F	M	F
Fredrick, Charles, carriage maker, res e Burgess.	1			
Fredrick, Jacob, carriage smith, " " -	1			
Fredrick, Thomas P., Jr., printer, " e Chestnut.	1	3		2
FINK, A. C., baggage master, B. & O. R.R. depot, residence w Vine street. - - - -	2	3	1	2
Fogwell, S. P., sewing machine agt., w Gambier, boards at Bergin House. - - - -	1			
Fogwell, Mrs., boards at Bergin House. - -		1		
Floyd, Thomas, stone mason, res w Gambier st. -	3	3	2	2
Flowers, Edwin, butcher with E. Rogers, resides at Gambier.				
First Ward School House, north side east Front, between McKenzie and McArthur streets.				
Fry, Simon, laborer, res Cemetery avenue. -	2	1	1	
Fry, John, cabinet maker, res Front & Mechanic.	1	2		1
Fowler, Benjamin, teamster, res w Gambier st.	1	2		1
Fowler, L. M., carpenter, res e Chestnut street. -	1	2		1
Fowler, Mattie, " " "				
Fowler, Herbert, dentist, " " " -	1			
FOWLER, A. C., carpenter and joiner, residence n Mulberry street. - - - - -	3	2	2	1
Fowler, Smith W., carpenter, res n Mulberry st.	1			
Fowler & Stephens, Dentists, Kirk Hall.				
FOWLER, C. R. (of the above firm,) residence north Mulberry street. - - - -	1	3		2
Fowles, John, huckster, res n Mulberry street. -	2	2	1	1
Fowles, Albert, butcher, " n Norton " -	1	1		
Fourth Ward School House, s side Sugar, between West and Norton streets.				
French, Thos., blacksmith, res Adams & Chestnut	1	1		
French, Mrs. Susan, " " " -		2		
French, John, blacksmith, res Railroad street. -	1	2		
French, M., teacher, res e Front street. - -	3	2	2	1
Fobes, William, carpenter, res e Front street. -	2	5	1	4
Fobes, P. R., saddler, " s Mulberry street.	1			
France, James, farmer, " e Chestnut " -	1	3		2
Franks, Mrs. Rose, " e High " -	4	2	4	1
First National Bank, n e cor Main & Vine streets. C. Delano, President; F. D. Sturges, Cashier; D. W. Lambert, Teller.				
Fifth Ward Engine House, cor Wooster & Main.				
Fifth Ward School House, west Plimpton street.				
Fisher, George, farmer, res e Front street. - -	1	2		1
Fisher, Hattie, " " "				
Fisher, Russell, clerk, " " " -	1			
Fisher, William, " " " -	1		1	
Feeney, James, Sr., laborer, res e Gambier street.	3	1	2	
Feeney, James, Jr., " " " " -	1			

C. A. BOPE,

Successor to A. Weaver,

—DEALER IN—

Foreign & Domestic Hardware,

Iron, Glass,

HORSE SHOES, HORSE NAILS,

Carriage Trimmings,

WAGON & BUGGY WOOD WORK,

MT. VERNON, OHIO.

—*ALSO*—

WHOLESALE AND RETAIL DEALER IN
ALL KINDS OF
COAL.

C. PETERMAN.   S. H. PETERMAN.

C. Peterman & Son,

— *DEALERS IN* —

DRY GOODS, NOTIONS,

COTTON YARN,

CARPET CHAIN, &c.

STORE—N. E. Corner Main & Gambier Sts.,

Mt. Vernon, Ohio.

Insure in the Companies represented	Popu-		Minors	
by — J. J. Fultz, Agt.	lation.			
	M	F	M	F
Feeney, Patrick, laborer, res e Plimpton street. -	6	5	5	4
Feaster, John A., carpenter, res e Gambier street.	1	1		
Frise, George P., cutter with Stauffer & Son, residence east High street. - -	1	1		
Flynn, John, laborer, res Coshocton avenue. -	3	2	2	1
Flynn, Martin, " " Railroad street. - -	1	1		
Flanagan, Patrick, laborer, res w Hamtramck st.	2	5	1	4
Flanagan, Elizabeth, res w Sugar street. - -		1		
FULTZ, J. J., Insurance Agent, office n w side Public Square, res n Mulberry street. -	3	2	2	
Farquhar, Mrs. Margaret, res n Jefferson street. -		3		1
Farnwold, Mary, res w High street. - -		1		
Farish, L. B., clerk, res Cemetery avenue. - -	1			
Farish, Mrs. M., " " " -		1		
Farrison, Harmon, produce packer, res Sandusky.	3	2	2	1
Farrar, James, bolt maker, res w Hamtramck st.	1	2		1
Fairchild, Lizzie, res Thistle Ridge. - -		1		
Fairchild, John S., tinner, res n Main street. -	1	1		
Fairchild, John L., clerk, " " -	1			
Fairchild, Frank L., (of the firm of C. & G. Cooper & Co.,) res Chicago.				
Fawcett, Mrs. Sarah, res e Plimpton street. - -		1		
Fawcett, Virginia E., teacher, res e Plimpton st.		1		
Fawcett, Maria L. " " -		1		
FISHBURN, A. M., confectioner, residence east Elizabeth street. - - - - - -	2	3	1	2
Fishburn, Wm. H., coachmaker, res e Elizabeth.	1			
Forsythe, Robert, shoemaker, res n Mulberry st.	1	2		1
FORDNEY, WILLIAM, Gas Collector & Carpenter, res n Mulberry street. - -	1			
Fordney, Sarah E., res n Mulberry street. - -		1		
Fordney, Margaret, " " " - -		1		
Fordney, Catharine, " " " - -		1		
Freelove, S. G., farmer, res Sandusky street. -	1	1		
Franklin, John, laborer, res w Hamtramck st. -	3	2	2	1
Ferguson, B. M., res w Hamtramck street. - -	1	3		1

G.

Gardner, Lester B., machinist, brds Bergin House	1	1		
Gardner, B. F., " res cor Gay & Burgess	2	2	1	1
Gardner, J. W., teamster, res Chester street. -	3	3	2	2
Garland, Mrs. Amanda, res w Front street. - -		1		
Garner, Patrick, machinist, res w Sugar street. -	1	1		
Gaffney, Patrick, laborer, res w High street. -	1			
GAY, JOHN F., Sheriff elect, residence corner Chesnut and Mechanic streets. - - -	1	1		

11

You can get Cash or Mutual Fire Insurance with   J. J. Fultz, Agt.

	Population. M | F	Minors M | F

	M	F	M	F
Garrard, William, Sr., laborer, res e High street.	3	1	2	
Garrard, William, Jr., " " " -	1			
Garrard, Jackson, " " " -	1			
Garrett, M. M., commercial traveler, res corner Main and Pleasant streets. - - - -	1	2		
GANTT, W. F., family grocer, n w cor High st. and Public Square, res cor Main & Burgess. -	3	2	2	1
Gantt, Minne, res cor Main & Burgess streets.				
Galena, Michael, peddler res Mansfield avenue. -	1	1		
Getner, George, yard master C. Mt. V. & C. R.R., residence e Water street. - - - -	2	1	1	
George, George, carpenter, res n Mulberry street.	4	1	3	
George, John, poney express, " " " -	1			
George, James, Sr., farmer, res Delaware road.				
George, James, Jr., works sash factory, res s Mechanic street. - - - - -	2	3	1	2
George, William, candy maker, s Main, res s Gay	4	2	3	1
George, John, baker, res s Main street. -	4	1	3	
George, Thomas, Policeman, res cor George & Oak	2	2	1	1
Gillaine, James, driver for Express Co., res e High	1			
GILCHRIST, J. H., clerk B. & O. R.R., residence cor Vine and Jefferson streets. - -	1			
Glaze, C. D., carpenter, res s Mulberry street. -	3	2	2	1
Glaze, Mrs. Anna, res Mansfield avenue. - -		2		
Glaze, Mrs. Elizabeth, res w High street. - -		1		
Graham, Mrs. Martha, res e High street. - -		2		
Graham, Della, res Young & Raymond's block. -		1		
Graham, D. C., plasterer, res e Curtis street. -	4	4	3	3
Graham, Mrs. Eliza, res n Main street. - -		1		
Graham & Critchfield, attorneys, Kirk Hall.				
GRAHAM, J. B., (of the above firm,) boards at the Bergin House. - - - -	1			
Graff & Carpenter, produce dealers, foot Main st.				
GRAFF, W. H., (of the above firm,) residence Mansfield avenue. - - - -	2	4	1	2
GRAFF, HEZEKIAH, carriage maker & blacksmith, w Front, res cor Front & Mulberry. -	2	3	1	2
Graff, Frank, carriage maker, res " "				
Graff, F. Eva, res " "				
Graff, Smith W., carriage trimmer, " -	1			
Graff, Jonathan, Sr., blacksmith, res e Front st, -	1	1		
Graff, Jonathan, Jr., carriage painter, res e Vine.	3	1	2	
GREER, H. H., attorney, post office building, residence e Gambier street. - - -	2	3	1	1
Greer, Millie, res " "				
GREER, B. A. F., Probate Judge, Court House, residence n Main street. - - - -	2	2	1	
Grant, Mary, residence w High street. - -		1		

A LITERARY CURIOSITY.

THE following sentence will attract the attention of the curious :

" *Sator arepo tenet opera rotas.*"

1. This spells backward and forward the same.
2. Then taking all the first letters of each word spells the first.
3. Then all the second letters of each word spells the second.
4. Then all the third and so on through the fourth and fifth.
5. Then commencing with the last letter of each word spells the last word.
6. Then the next to the last of each word, and so on through.

Insure Yourselves and Property with	Popu-		Minors	
J. J. FULTZ, Agent.	lation.			
	M	F	M	F

GRANT, ISAAC, residence north Gay street. -	1	1		
Grant, Sophia, residence n Gay street. - - -		1		
GRANT, BENJAMIN, residence corner Main and Pleasant streets. - - - - -	3	3	2	1
Gray, Martha, residence s Mulberry street. - -		1		
Gray, Mrs. Priscilla, res cor Chestnut & Mechanic		2		
Grieff, Peter, laborer, res cor High & Mulberry sts	1			
GREGORY, C. P., gunsmith, e Gambier, residence w High street. - - - - -	2	1	1	
Gregory, Wm., fireman, C. Mt. V. & C. res w High	1	1		
GREEN, ISRAEL, Druggist, s Main, near Gambier, res s Mulberry street. - - - - -	2	3	1	1
Green, Harry M., druggist, res s Mulberry street.				
Green, Delia, " " " "				
Griley, John, barber, boards Central House. -	1			
Grim, Robert, boiler maker, res Cemetery avenue	1	2		
Grim, Isaiah, plasterer, res Railroad street. -	1	4		3
Grim, Charles, laborer, " " " . -		1		
Groeell, E., " " w Sugar " -	5	1	4	
Gow, William, painter, " Cemetery avenue. -	2	2	1	1
Gower, William, laborer, C. Mt. V. & C. R. R., residence w Wooster street. - - - -	2	3	1	1
Gotshall, David, farmer, res w Sugar street. -	3	5	2	4
Gotshall, John P., " " Granville road.				
Gotshall, Samuel R., student, " "				
Gotshall, John S., " "				
Gotshall, Florence, " " .				
GORDON, JOSEPH C., physician, post office building, res corner Sugar and Mechanic sts.	1	3		2
Grubb, Isaac, student, res n Mulberry street. -	1			
Grubb, David Z, clerk, " e Vine street. - -	2	2	1	1
Grubb, Mary, seamstress, res s Main street. - -		1		
Guernsey, Abraham, res w Vine street. - -	2	4	1	3
Guillian, Mrs. Sarah, res cor High & West streets		1		
Guy, John, farmer, res Utica road.				

H

HARPER, L., editor "Mt. Vernon Democratic Banner," res e Gambier street. - - -	3	2	2	1
Harper, Katie, " " " .				
Harper, Frank, student, res e Gambier street.				
Harper, Jack, druggist, " " "				
Harper, W. M., local editor Banner, res e Gambier	1			
Harper, Howard, Banner Job Printer, res e Vine.	2	1	1	
Harper, Clarence B., printer, res e Gambier street	1			

	Population		Minors	
	M	F	M	F
Harnwell, Mrs. Adam, res e Gambier street. -		1		
Harrington, Mrs. Caroline, res s Gay street. - -		3		2
Hart, Abel, Sr., carpenter, res corner Gambier & McArthur streets. - - - -	1			
HART, ABEL, Jr., attorney, over Errett's stove store, s Main. Member Ohio House of Rep. Residence cor Gambier & McArthur streets. -	2	2	1	1
Hart, Wm. R., carriage trimmer, res e High st. -	1	1		
Hart, Fred. James, clerk, " " -	1			
Hartnoll, John, cabinet maker, res w Vine street.	1	2		1
Harmon, Rachel, help at Rowley House. - -		1		
Harris, John, farmer, res w Chestnut street. -	2	1	1	
Harrold, Nardo, horse trainer, brds Rowley House	1			
HARDING, THOMAS, Coal Dealer, residence w Hamtramck street. - - - -	1	3		1
Harker, Thos., poney express, res w Hamtramck	2	1	1	
Hardesty, John, farmer, res Sandusky street. -	4	2	3	1
Hadley, Isaac, residence e Vine street. - -	2	2	1	1
Hadley, Eva, " "				
Hadley, Lester, tinner, res " " - -	1	1		
HALLEY, J. C., dentist, Braddock building, s Main, boards at Mrs. Buckland's, s Main st.	1			
Hall, J. M., millwright, res e High street. - -	2	4	1	2
Hall, Mrs. Nancy, res s Mechanic street. -		1		
Haller, Newton, carpenter, res s McArthur street.	3	1	2	
Haller, Joseph T., painter, res n Main street. -	2	2	1	1
Halsey, D. F., farmer, res Columbus & Sparta road				
Hanna, Wm. Alex., book keeper, res n Norton st	3	3	2	2
Hancock, George, brick & stone mason, res w Vine	2	3	1	2
Hanger, William, boiler maker, res e Chestnut st.	1			
Hanagan, Patrick, section boss, C. Mt. V. & C. R. R., res e Water street. - - - -	5	4	4	3
HAMILTON, J. H., editor "Mt. Vernon Republican," res cor Gay and Lamartin streets.	1	2		1
Hamilton, Mary, res " " "				
Hamilton, E. C., local ed. Republican, res n Gay.	2	1	1	
Hawley, Mrs. Maria E., res n Norton street. -	1	3	1	2
Hauk, Mrs. G. W., res e Gambier street. -		2		1
Hauk, Laura, " " "				
Haymes, John D., baker, shop and res e Water st	3	2	2	1
Haymes, Frank, baker, res e Water street. - -	1			
Hayes, Michael, moulder, res Coshocton avenue.	3	3	2	2
Hayes, Margaret, res Coshocton avenue.				
Hayes, Mary, brds at W. S. Hydes', Mansfield ave.				
Hayes, Katie, brds at D. B. Kirk's w Chesnut st.				
Hayes, Thomas, clerk with Jas. Rogers, w Vine, res w Hamtramck street. - - -	1		1	
Hackley, David, [c] laborer, res n Mulberry st. -	3	3	2	2

Insure Yourselves in the C. M. L. & H. I. Co., of Mt. Vernon, O.

	Population		Minors	
	M	F	M	F
Hackley, John, [c] laborer, res e High street. -	2	4	1	1
Helms, Wm. P., poney express, res n Main st. -	1	2		1
Henderson, William, hatter, res e Front street. -	1	4		3
Henderson, Anna, res e Front street.				
Henderson, Carrie, " " "				
Henderson, Ella, sales lady, res e Front street.				
Henderson, David, butcher, " " "	1			
HENEGAN, JOHN, railroad contractor, residence cor High and McArthur streets. -	4	4	3	3
Henegan, Mary Jane, res High and McArthur sts				
Henegan, Katie, " " "				
Henegan, Belle, " " "				
Henegan, John, Jr., " " "				
Henegan, Frank, " " "				
Henegan, Mrs. William, " "		1		
HENLEY, PATRICK, restaurant, near B. & O. depot, res cor Vine and Adams streets. - -	2	4	1	3
Headington, George, laborer, res Granville road.				
Headington, Thompson, moulder, res s Mulberry	3	2	2	1
Headington, J. N., County Surveyor, office rear Court House, res Centerburgh.				
Heavyman, Mark, moulder, res w Gambier st. -	3	2	2	1
Hildreth, Charles M., wool buyer, res w Gambier	1			
Hildreth, Mrs. John, res cor Gambier & Mechanic		1		
Hildreth, Mrs. C. G., " " "	2	1	2	
Hildreth, Wash., teamster, cor Vine & Mechanic.	1			
Hildreth, Nancy, res s Mulberry street. - -		1		
Hildreth, Ruth, " " "		1		
Hilliar, Thomas, farmer, residence Gambier road.				
Hilliar, A. F., carpenter & builder, " "				
Hilliar, G. W., farmer, residence " "				
Hersh, Levi, carpenter, " e High street. -	2	3	1	2
Herrod, Wm., organ dealer, res e Curtis street. -	1	2		1
Held, William, moulder, res Jefferson & Chestnut	1	3		2
Hincken, Savilla, help at Bergin House. - -		1		
Higgins, Rufus, laborer, res cor Mulberry & High	2	1	1	
Hickman, Thomas, boiler maker, res w Wooster.	1	4		2
HINDELL, THOMAS, machinist, residence east Front street. - - - - - -	1			
Hills, H. C., dealer in queensware, &c., s Main st res n Main street. - - - -	1	2		
Hill, Edward, marble cutter, res n Mulberry st. -	1	2		1
Hill, J. Monroe, carpenter, res n West street. -	2	3	1	2
Hill, John, [c] laborer, res w Sugar street. -	1			
Hill, Mrs. Lydia, res Monroe street. - -		1		
Hill, John, musician, res Harkness road.				
Hill, Percival, carpenter, cor Jefferson & Sugar.	2	1	1	
Hill, Edwin, " " " -	2	1	1	

Insurance against loss from Fire and Lightning, by the Mt. Vernon M. & N-B. Insurance Agency.	Popu-lation.		Minors	
	M	F	M	F
HILL, N. N., sec'y. Gas Co., cor Main & Gambier streets, res n Main street. - - - -	1	1		
Hill, Mrs. Ellen, [c] res w Vine street. - - -	2	3	2	2
Hopkins, Daniel, laborer, res s Mechanic street. -	2	3	1	2
Hopkins, James, farmer, res Harkness road.				
Hogan, Michael, peddler, res w Chestnut street. -	3	3	2	2
Hogle, Martin, brick maker, res e Elizabeth st. -	2	1	1	
Hogle, William, " " " - -	1	1		
Hogle, Mrs. Eph., residence Calhoun street. -	1	2	1	
Hogle, Mrs. Amelia M., res Sandusky street. -		2		
Hogle, Charles L., huckster, res " " -	1			
Hogle, Eph., brick maker, res " " -	2		1	
Hogle, Frank, painter, res e Chestnut street. -	1	2		1
Hoover, Israel, marble dealer, res w Gambier st.	1	2		
Hoover, Elmira, res w Gambier street.				
HORNER, WM. J., agent United States & Union Express Cos., res e High street. - - -	2	1	1	
Horner, Obediah, brakeman, C. Mt. V. & C. RR. res e Front street. - - - -	1	1		
Hoey, William C., res Mansfield avenue. - -	1			
Hoey, Miss Frank, " " " - -		1		
Hook, Ezra, farmer, res " " - -	1	2		
Hopwood, Mrs. Samuel, res e Gambier street. -	2	3	2	
Hopwood, Taomas, carpenter, res " " -	1			
House, T., C. Mt. V. & C. R. R., res cor Front & Compromise streets. - - - -	3	2	2	
Hopper, John, laborer, res w High street. -	2	2	1	1
Hockstrasser, Edward, barber, brds Central House	1			
Hoke, Peter, farmer & stock dealer, res e High st.	1	4		2
Hoke, Mary, res e High street.				
Hodges, Geo. H., medical student res e Chestnut.	1			
Hodgins, Lena K., teacher, res e High street. -		1		
Hood, Mrs. Maria L., res Chestnut & Coshocton. -		1		
Hood, Miss Frank, teacher, " " -		1		
Hook and Ladder Co., e side Gay between High and Chestnut streets.				
Hurd, Mrs. R. C., residence n Main street. -		3		2
Hunt, Thomas, carpenter, res e High street. -	4	3	3	1
Hunt, William, boiler maker, res Coshocton ave.	1	2		
Hunt, John, teamster, res s Mulberry street. -	1			
Hunt, Frank, porter at Rowley House. -	1			
Hunt, John, laborer, res s Mulberry street. -	1	2		
Hunt, Edward, moulder, res " " -	1			
Hunt, Ezra, laborer, res w Vine street. -	2	3	1	2
Hunt, Mrs. Mary, " " " -		1		
Hunt, John, grocer, w High st., res Sugar & West	1	3		1
Hunt, Nellie, res corner Sugar and West streets. -				
Hunt, Annie, " " " " "				

Insure in the Companies represented *by* J. J. Fultz, Agt.	Population.		Minors	
	M	F	M	F
HUNT, L. G., propr. Hunt's Omnibus Line, res s McKenzie street. - - - -	1	2		
Hunt, Richard, carpenter, res e Gambier. - -	1	1		
Huntsberry, Uriah, res Sandusky street. - -	3	3	2	2
Huntsberry, James, varnisher, res Sandusky st.	1			
Huntsberry, Mrs. James, res e Gambier street. -		2		
Huntsberry, L. E., assessor 1st Ward, res e Gambier street. - - - - -	1			
Huntsberry, Milo K., printer, res e Gambier st. -	1			
Hull, R. S., clerk, res Mansfield avenue. - -	1			
Hull, Joseph teamster, res " " - -	1			
Hull, George, laborer, " " " - -	1			
Hull, Mrs. Eliza, " " " - -		3		1
Hull, Mary, " " "				
Hull, Ella, boards at Dr. Pickard's, w High st.				
Hutchinson. Mrs. Mary, res n Mulberry street. -		2		1
HUTCHINSON, JAMES, boot and shoe store, s Main street, res cor Gambier & Gay streets. -	1	2		
Hutchinson, James B., res s McKenzie street. -	1			
Huston, William, clerk, res Gambier & Mechanic	1	1		
Huston, John, carpenter, res Front & Mechanic. -	1	3		
Huston, Emma, " " "				
Huston, Belle, " " "				
Hutton, Charles, produce packer, res e Elizabeth.	1	4	3	
Hutton, Hugh, moulder, res w Pleasant street. -	1			
Hutton, Mrs. John, " " " -		3	2	
Hughes, A., farmer, res Martinsburgh road.				
Hughes, Isaac, tavern keeper, junction Columbus and Newark roads.				
Hughes, J. A., marble cutter, brds at J. Sapp's. -	1			
Hughes, George, farmer, res Pleasant township.				
Hurlburt, L., produce packer, res n Mulberry st.	1	3	2	
Hurley, John C., [c] laborer, res w Vine street. -	1			
HUBBELL, O. W., contractor and builder, residence w High street. - - - -	1	2		1
Hubbell, Mary, res w High street.				
Hyatt, Mrs. Rispah, res Mulberry & Hamtramck		1		
HYDE, JOSHUA, jeweler, Woodward block, res cor High and McArthur streets. - -	3	3	2	1
Hyde, C. C., jeweler, res High & McArthur sts. -	1			
HYDE, W. S., Clerk Court Common Pleas, residence Mansfield avenue. - - -	2	2	1	1

I

Israel & Koons, attorneys, Israel's block, n Main.				
Israel, Samuel, (of the above firm,) res n Main. -	1	6		2

12

National Conventions.

Prior to 1832, Presidential Candidates were selected by Congressional and Legislative Caucuses, or by State Conventions and by public meetings. The first *National* Convention was held by the Democratic party at Baltimore, May 22, 1832.

1832 - The *First* Democratic Convention held at Baltimore, May 22.—Nominated Andrew Jackson.

1835 - The *Second* Democratic Convention held at Baltimore, May 20.—Nominated Martin Van Buren.

This year the Whigs nominated Henry Clay by public meetings held in Ohio, Pennsylvania and other states. The Anti-Masons nominated William Wirt, of Md.

1839—The *First* Whig Convention, Harrisburg, Dec. 4—Harrison.

1840—The *Third* Democratic, Baltimore, May 24—Van Buren.

1844—The *Fourth* Democratic, Baltimore, May 27—J. K. Polk.

1844 - The *Second* Whig, Baltimore, May 1—Henry Clay.

1848 - The *Third* Whig, Philadelphia, June —, —Gen. Taylor.

1848—The *Fifth* Democratic, Baltimore, May —, —Lewis Cass.

1852 - The *Sixth* Democratic, Baltimore, June 1—Frank. Pierce.

1852 - The *Fourth* Whig, Baltimore, June 15—Gen. Scott.

1856—The *Seventh* Democratic, Cincinnati, June 2—J. Buchanan.

1856—The *First* Republican, Philadelphia, June 17—J.C. Fremont.

1860—The *Second* Republican, Chicago, May 17—A. Lincoln.

1860 - The *Eighth* Democratic, Charleston, S. C., April 23—After a session of 9 days, and more than 50 ballots, the Convention adjourned to meet at Baltimore, June 15. At Baltimore a portion of the delegates seceded from the regular Convention, and nominated John C. Breckenridge, of Ky. The regulars nominated Stephen A. Douglas, of Illinois. John Bell, of Tennessee, was nominated by the Constitutional Union party.

1864—The *Third* Republican, Baltimore, June 8—A. Lincoln.

1864 - The *Ninth* Democratic, Chicago, Aug, 30—G. B. McClellan.

1868—The *Tenth* Democratic, New York, July 4—H. Seymour.

1868— The *Fourth* Republican, Chicago, May 21—U. S. Grant.

1872—The *Fifth* Republican, Philadelphia, June 5—U. S. Grant.

1872 - The *Eleventh* Democratic, Baltimore, July 9—H. Greeley. Mr. Greeley had been previously nominated by the Liberal Republican Convention at Cincinnati, May 1.

1876—The *Sixth* Republican, Cincinnati, June 14—R. B. Hayes·

1876—The *Twelfth* Democratic, St. Louis, June 27—S. J. Tilden.

	Popu- lation.		Minors	
Insure Yourselves and Property with *J. J. FULTZ, Agent.*	M	F	M	F

Israel, Amanda, res n Main street.
Israel, Lavina, " " "
Israel, James, proprietor oil mill, res n Main st. | 2 | 1 | 1 |
ISRAEL, SAMUEL H., Cashier Knox County
  Savings Bank, Israel's block, res n Main st. - | 1 |
IRVINE, JAMES C., butcher, Rowley House,
  residence e Gambier street. - - - | 1 | 3 |
Irvine, Martha, res e Gambier street.
Irvine, Rebecca, " " "
Irvine & Cooper's Restaurant, s Main, near Ber-
  gin House. | | | 1 |
IRVINE, J. J., (of the above firm,) residence
  Clinton township.
IRVINE, CLARK, Prosecuting Attorney, office
  rear Court House, res cor Mulberry & Gambier | 1 |
IRVINE, EUGENE, Restaurant, s Main, near
  Rowley House, res cor Mulberry and Gambier. | 1 |
Irvine, Milan, clerk, res " " | 1 |
Irvine, Mrs. Matilda, " " " | | 5 | | 4 |
Irvine, Hortense, " " "
Irvine, Rosabel, " " "
Irvine, Ada, " " "
Irvine, Mrs. John, res w Front street. - - - | | 2 |
Irvine, Angeline, res s McArthur street. - - | | 1 |
Iams, F. M., Pastor Baptist Church, res e Vine st | 4 | 3 | 3 | 1 |
Iams, Mary, res e Vine street.
Iams, Nellie, " " "
Ingram, Mrs. Hannah, res cor Front & McKenzie | | 4 |
Ingram, Martha, " " "
Ingram, Etta, " " "
INGRAM, A. B., Deputy Revenue Collector,
  e side Public Square, res Front & McKenzie. - | 2 | 2 | 1 | 1 |

J

JONES, Gen. G. A., Superintendent C. Mt. V.
  & C. R.R., residence cor High & Sandusky sts | 2 | 3 | 1 | 2 |
Jones, Fred. W., Road Master, C. Mt. V. & C. RR.
  residence e Front street. - - - | 2 | 3 | 1 | 2 |
Jones, Mrs. Mary E., res e Chestnut street. - | 1 | 2 | 1 | 1 |
Jones, Thomas, teamster, res e Burgess street. - | 1 | 3 | | 2 |
Jones, Lorenzo, laborer, res Calhoun street. - - | 2 | 1 | 1 |
Jones, Frank. " " " " | 1 | 2 | | 1 |
Jacobs, B. F., stone mason, res e Curtis street. - | 3 | 1 | 2 |
Jacobs, Joseph, chair maker, res Vine & Walnut. | 1 | 2 |
Jackson & Alling, restaurant, nr B. & O. R.R. Dpt
JACKSON, HARVEY, (of the above firm,) res
  cor Vine and Jefferson streets. - - - | 4 | 4 | 3 | 1 |

CONGRESS.—SPEAKERS OF THE HOUSE.

1789—Frederick A. Muhlenberg, of Pennsylvania.
1791—Jonathan Trumbull, of Connecticut.
1793—Frederick A. Muhlenberg, of Pennsylvania.
1795—Jonathan Dayton, of New Jersey, (2 Congresses.)
1799—Theodore Sedgwick, of Massachusetts.
1801—Nathaniel Macon, of North Carolina, (3 Congresses.)
1807—Joseph B. Varnum, of Massachusetts, (2   "   )
1811—Henry Clay, of Kentucky, (5 Congresses.)
1821—Philip P. Barbour, of Virginia.
1823—Henry Clay, of Kentucky.
1825—John W. Taylor, of New York.
1827—Andrew Stephenson, of Virginia, (3 Congresses.)
1834—John Bell, of Tennessee.
1835—James K. Polk, of Tennessee, (2 Congresses.)
1839—Robert M. T. Hunter, of Virginia.
1841—John White, of Kentucky.
1843—John W. Jones, of Virginia.
1845—John W. Davis, of Indiana.
1847—Robert C. Winthrop, of Massachusetts.
1849—Howell Cobb, of Georgia.
1851—Lynn Boyd, of Kentucky, (2 Congresses.)
1856—Nathaniel P. Banks, of Massachusetts.
1857—James L. Orr, of South Carolina.
1860—William Pennington, of New Jersey.
1861—Galusha A. Gow, of Pennsylvania.
1863—Schuyler Colfax, of Indiana, (3 Congresses.)
1869—Theodore M. Pomeroy, of New York.
1869—James G. Blaine, of Maine, (3 Congresses.)
1875—Michael C. Kerr, of Indiana.
1876—Samuel S. Cox, of New York, (pro. tem.)
1876—Milton Saylor, of Ohio, (pro. tem.)

PARTY NAMES.

1796.—The parties were known and designated as Federalists and Democrats.
1824.—Parties were designated as Federalists, Democrats, Whigs.
1826.—Democrats, Whigs, Anti-Masons.
1828.—Democrats and Whigs.
1848—Democrats, Whigs, and Free Soilers.
1856.—Democrats, Whigs, and Native Americans.
1860.—Democrats and Union Republicans.
1864.—Democrats and Republicans.

Insurance against loss from Fire and Lightning, by the Mt. Vernon M. & N-B. Insurance Agency.	Popu-lation.		Minors	
	M	F	M	F
Jackson, Annie, milliner, res Vine & Jefferson.				
Jackson, S. H., carriage maker, res w Vine street.	3	4	2	3
Jackson, Mrs. William, res w Chestnut street. -		1		
Jackson, William, laborer, res " " -	1			
Jackson, Saint, baker, shop and res n Main street	2	1	1	
Jackson, James, [c] barber, res e Vine street. -	2	3	1	2
Jackson, Mrs. Sarah, res n Gay street. - -	1	1	1	
Janes, E. C., telegraph operator, C. Mt. V. & C. R.R. Depot, boards at Mrs. Buckland's. -	1			
Jennings, John, brick mason, res w Chestnut st.	1	1		
Jennings, John G., clerk, res w " -	1			
JENNINGS, H. W., merchant, (of the firm of Ringwalt & Jennings,) res e Vine street.	2	4	1	2
Jenkins, Nathaniel, farmer, res Green Valley road.				
Jenkins, Riley, [c] laborer, res w Chestnut street.	2	1	1	
Jenkins, W. H., [c] teamster, res w " " -	1			
Jimeson, William, broom maker, res e Sugar st.	2	3	1	
Jimeson, Charles, " " " " -	1			
JOHNSON, RICHARD M., tinner, residence e Sugar street. - - - - -	2	4	1	2
Johnson, Mrs. Effie, res e Sugar street. - -		1	.	
Johnson, Richard, laborer, res e Vine street. -	1	1		
Johnson, James, farmer, res Columbus road.				
Johnson, Oak, " " " "				
Johnson, Isaac, " " " "				
Johnson, Peter, laborer, res e High street. - -	1	3		1
Johnson, Willis, marble cutter, res e Vine street.	2	1	1	
Johnston, H. H., grocer, (of the firm of Updegraff & Johnston, Pub. Sqr.) res w Chestnut st. -	2	2	1	
Johnston, Mrs. M. E., res e Chestnut street. -	1	2	1	
Jordon, W. S., machinist, res w High street. -	3	1	2	

K

Knox County Mutual Insurance Co., e High street				
Knox County National Bank, n w cor Main st. & Public Square.—Henry B. Curtis, President. John M. Ewalt, Cashier. E. W. Pyle, teller.				
Kaiser, Frank, laborer, res Round Hill. - -	2	4	1	2
Kaiser, Adam, farmer, res Columbus road.				
Kaiser, John, " " " "				
Keller, George F., brewer, res Rogers street. -	1	1		
Keller, George, teamster, res e Gambier street. -	1	2		
Keller, William " " " " -	1			
KELLER, C., produce dealer, n Mulberry street, residence n Main street. - - -	1	1		
Keller, John, produce packer, res n Mulberry st.	2	2	1	1

Insure Yourselves in the C. M. L. & H. I. Co., of Mt. Vernon, O.	Population.		Minors	
	M	F	M	F
Kelly, Patrick, laborer, res w Gambier street. -	1	1		
Kelly, Michael, farmer, " " " -	4	1	3	
Kelly, Hugh, grocer, n Main, res Coshocton ave.	2	2	1	1
Kelly, Andrew, res e High street. - - -	2	3	1	2
Kelly, Frank, clerk, res " " - - -	1			
Kelly, John P. & Co., dealers in hardware, nails, &c., e side Public Square.				
KELLY, JOHN P., (of the above firm,) res w Burgess street. - - - - -	1	1		
Kelly, Jeff., machinist, res w Pleasant street. -	3	2	2	
Kelly, William, moulder, res n West street. -	1	4		3
Kelly, Thomas, machinist, res Sandusky street. -	1			
Kelly, J. Harvey, " " " -	1			
Kelly, Mrs. C. A., res " " -		2		1
Kelly, Mathias, grocer, cor Vine & Mulberry sts. residence same building. - - -	5	2	4	1
KELSEY, C. M., Surgeon Dentist, office and residence north Main street. - - -	1	1		
Kelsey, Edward Silliman, medical student, residence north Main street. - - -	1			
Keyes, George W., laborer, res e Gambier street.	1			
Keigley, Morgan, huckster, res Sandusky street.	1			
Keefer, Daniel, " res n Mulberry street	1	3		2
Keefer, Al., " res e Curtis street. -	1	2		1
Keefer, Henry, farmer, res Columbus road.				
Keene, Mrs. Deborah, res s Mulberry street. -		1		
Kerr, Benjamin, farmer, res nr Martinsburg road				
Kerr, A. S., sample room, Rowley House. -	1			
Kerr, Mrs. Eva, res e Vine street. - - -		1		
Kerr, Thomas, res Clinton township.				
Kenney, E. C., night operator, B. & O. R.R., residence cor Vine and Jefferson streets. -	1		1	
Keefe, Mrs. Mary, res w High street. -		1		
Keeley, James C., shoemaker, w Vine, res w High	2	1	1	
Kester, Frank, res Cemetery avenue. - -	1	1		
Kidwell, Edward, stone mason, res s Catharine.	3	4	2	2
Kidwell, Carrie, res s Catharine street.				
Kindrick, Mrs. Nancy, res Sugar and Mulberry.		2		
Kindrick & Norton, Milliners, s Main street.				
Kindrick, Miss Sarah, (of the above firm,) residence cor Sugar and Mulberry streets. -		1		
KINDRICK, R. N., dealer in Cigars, Tobacco, &c., s Main, res Mansfield avenue. - -	2	1	1	
Kindrick, J. Frank, res "	1			
Kingston, Ezekiel, machinist, res n Norton street	2	2	1	1
King, Henry H., cabinet maker, res s " "	1	2		1
King, Johnston, " " " w Gambier.	1	2		
King, William L., farmer, res Clinton township.				

Insure against Fire and Lightning. *J. J. Fultz, Agt.*	Popu-lation.		Minors	
	M	F	M	F
King, William M., farmer, res Clinton township.				
Kilkenny, Edward, boiler maker, res Railroad st	1	3		2
Kilkenny, Mrs. Mary, res Sandusky street. - -		2		
Kilkenny, Rose, " " "				
Knight, Mrs. H. B., res Madison street. - -	1	1	1	
Kirk & McIntire, attorneys, n Main street.				
Kirk, D. B., (of the above firm,) res cor Sugar & Mulberry streets. - - - - -	1	4		3
KIRK, ROBERT C., Revenue Collector, No. 1, Kremlin, res e Gambier street. - - -	2	2	1	
Kirk, G. P., clerk, collector's office, res e Gambier	1			
Kneelen, Hamilton, shoemaker, res w Gambier.	6	4	5	3
Kneelen, Nellie, help at Central House. - -		1		
Knode, Neil, residence w Front street. - -	1	3		2
Koons & Israel, attorneys, Israel's block, n Main.				
KOONS, WM. M., (of the above firm,) City So-licitor, res cor McKenzie & Elizabeth streets.	1	1		
Koons, Mrs. Elizabeth, res " " "		1		
KOONS, C. W., engineer Fire steamer, resi-dence Council building, n Gay street. - -	1	1		
Kokosing Iron Works, T. L. Clark, lessee, foot of Main street.				
Kokosing Steam Flouring Mills, Tudor & Stevens, lessees, foot of Main street.				
KRAFFT, FRED., blacksmith, w Wooster, resi-dence cor Wooster and Mulberry streets. -	5	3	4	2
KUNKELL, SAMUEL, law student, with Gen. Morgan, res n Mulberry street. - - -	1			

L

Lantz, O. M., printer, res n Main street. - -	1			
Lane, John M., pattern maker, res Mansfield ave	3	5	2	4
Lane, P. C., carpenter, res Chester street. - -	2	2	1	
Lane, Louis, student, " " "				
Lane, William, carpenter, res Sandusky street. -	3	2	2	1
Lane, Charles R., " " " " -	1	2		1
Lane, P. E., " " " " -	1	3		1
Lane, James A., brick mason, res e Chestnut st. -	2	3	1	1
Lane, Mary, teacher, res e Chestnut street. - -		1		
Lane, James T., brick mason, res e Chestnut st. -	1	3		2
Lane, David C., " " " -	1			
Lang, William, laborer, res Coshocton avenue. -	3	1	2	
Lambert, Mrs. Harvey, res cor Division & High.		2		
LAMBERT, D. W., Teller 1st National Bank, residence e High street. - - - - -	1	2		
Lambert, William, laborer, res e Chestnut street.	3	1	2	

You can get Cash or Mutual Fire Insurance with J. J. Fultz, Agt.	Popu-lation.		Minors	
	M	F	M	F
Lamson, James, painter, res e Vine street. - -	5	3	4	1
Lafever, Minor, farmer, res Kinney road.				
Lafever, Urania, " "				
Lafever, Mary, " "				
Lafever, Samuel, farmer, res near Columbus road				
LAFEVER, ISAAC, Jr., farmer, res Delaware road.				
Lafever, Chambers, laborer, res s Gay street. -	1	2		1
Lafever, Ida, res s Gay street.				
Lafever, William, butcher, res w Front street. -	1			
Lafever, Price, farmer, res Lafever road.				
Lafever, Abe, butcher, w Vine, res w Front st. -	2	1	1	
Lafever, Charles, tailor, res Sandusky street. -	1		1	
Latham, Jerry, [c] teamster, res w High street. -	2	1	1	
Larrison, Andrew, tailor, brds Rowley House. -	1			
Larimore, F. C., physician and surgeon, office s Main, over Green's drug store, res n Main.	2	1	1	
Larimore, Mrs. L., res e Chestnut, near Main. -		1		
Larimore, Lucy, teacher, res " " "		1		
Lauderbaugh, John K., assessor 3d ward, res east Chestnut street. - - - - -	3	3	2	2
Lauderbaugh, Hugh, plasterer, res e High street.	2	3	1	2
Lauderbaugh, Mrs. Andrew, " " -		2		1
Lauderbaugh, Charles, plasterer, " " -	1			
Lawson, Andrew, tailor, brds Bergin House. -	1			
LEWIS, FRIENDY, saddle and harness maker, res e High street. - - - - - -	2	4	1	2
Lewis, Hester Ann, res e High street.				
Lewis, Ollie May, " "				
Lewis, John, [c] barber, res n Gay street. - -	2	3	1	2
Lewis Mrs. Mary, [c] " " - -		1		
Lewis, David, well digger, res n Norton street. -	1	2		1
Lewis, John N., Chief Engineer C. Mt. V. and C. R.R., res w High street. - - -	1	2		
Lewis, Annie, res " "				
Lewis, James, newspaper agent, res w High st. -	1			
LEWIS, DAVID C., City Civil Engineer, res cor Norton and Chestnut streets. - - -	2	3	1	
Lewis, Alice, res cor Norton and Chestnut streets.				
Lewis, Mary, " " " "				
Lewis, Clifford, " " " "				
Lewis, Sidney, laborer, res w Gambier street. -	2	3	1	2
Lewis, George B., machinist, res " " -	2	3	1	2
Lewis, Solomon, res w Gambier street. - -	1	2		1
Lewis, L. H., clerk, res e Burgess street. - -	1	1		
Lewis, Lizette, brds with Mrs. A. Weaver, e High		1		
Leonard, Martin, brick mason, res n West street.	3	2	2	1
Leonard, William H., help at Bergin House. -	1			

Insure in the Companies represented by *J. J. Fultz, Agt.*	Population M	F	Minors M	F
Leonard, Mrs. Bridget, res cor West & Burgess. -		1		
LEOPOLD, MAX, Clothier, Woodward block, Main and Vine sts., res cor Vine and Gay sts.	3	3	2	1
Lennon & Dunbar, attorneys, s Main, Eli Miller's block.				
LENNON, JOHN J., (of the above firm,) residence east Front street. - - - - -	1	1		
Lee, John, laborer, res e Burgess street. - -	2	2	1	1
Lee, Michael, machinist, res e Plimpton street. -	4	2	3	1
Lee, Thomas, huckster, res Railroad street. - -	2	2	1	1
Lee, John C., proprietor Central House, Pub. Sqr.	3	3	2	2
Leferre, William, laborer, res Railroad street. -	3	2	2	
Leferre, Benjamin, " " " " -	1			
LEVERING, JOHN C., County Commissioner, address Levering Post Office, Knox county, O.				
Leyden, Bridget, res w Sugar street. - -		1		
Lawler, James, works Oil Mill, res n Gay street.	4	3	3	2
LAWLER, JOHN, machinist, residence Sandusky street. - - - - - -	3	5	2	4
Lawrence, Allen, plasterer, res e Gambier street.	1			
Licklider, Mrs. ——, res Sandusky street. -	3	2	3	1
Licklider, Mary, at G. E. Raymond's, w High st.		1		
Lindsey, Charles, [c] teamster, res w Vine street.	2	1	1	•
Lindsey, John M., res w Front street. - -	1	1		
Linn, John, res cor Chestnut and West streets. -	1			
Lind, Philip, miller, res s Norton street. - -	2	2	1	1
Linsted, T. W., machinist, res cor Gay & Burgess	1	1		
Lingerfield, Henry, laborer, res Sandusky street.	3	2	2	1
Laughery, J. K., blacksmith, res e Front street. -	2	2	1	
Laughery, Elizabeth Jane, " " "				
Lippitt & Shrimplin, Druggists, west Vine street.				
Lippitt, B. F., (of the above firm,) res w Sugar st	2	1	1	
Lippitt, Lloyd B., res w Vine street. - -	2	4	1	3
Lucas, Ella, seamstress, res Sandusky street. -		1		
Lucas, Sarah, [c] res s Gay street. - - -		1		
Laurants, Mary H., help at Bergin House. -		1		
Lore, John, farmer, res Mansfield avenue. -	1			
Logsden, John, teamster, res s Division street. -	1	1		
Logsden, George J., painter, res s "	1			
Logsden, Lloyd E., carpenter, " " -	2	1	1	
Logsden, James W., painter, " " -	1			
Logsden, Mrs. James W., res Sandusky street. -	2	1	2	
Lobach, Henry, trader, res e Chestnut street. -	4	6	3	5
Lobach, Rodolph, carpenter, res " " -	1			
Long, John, laborer, res w Vine street. - -	3	1	2	
Long, Ollie, sales lady at W.C.Sapp's, res Water st		1		
Loveridge, William, farmer, res Wooster road.				
Loveridge, Aaron, " " w Chestnut st. -	1	1		

13

THE PRESIDENTIAL ELECTORS.

AT the first and second elections (1788 and 1792) all the electors appointed voted for Washington, who was the only President ever chosen by an unanimous vote. At the third election (1796) 139 electors were appointed, 71 of whom voted for John Adams and 68 of whom voted for Thomas Jefferson—electing Adams by a majority of only *two votes*. The electors did not divide by States or "colleges," as is shown by these facts: The people in North Carolina appointed 12 electors; 11 of them voted for Jefferson and 1 for Adams. In Virginia 21 electors were appointed: 20 voted for Jefferson and 1 for Adams. Of the 11 electors appointed in Maryland, 4 voted for Jefferson and 7 for Adams. Of the 15 appointed in Pennsylvania, 14 voted for Jefferson and 1 for Adams.

At the fourth election (1800) occurred the famous contest between Jefferson and Burr, each of whom received 73 votes, given by electors appointed in nine States. The 12 electors of New York, the 21 of Virginia, the 4 of Kentucky, the 3 of Tennessee, the 8 of South Carolina, and the 4 of Georgia, all voted solidly for *both*, intending that one should be President and the other Vice President, but not expressing any choice between them. The 15 electors of Pennsylvania gave to each of them 8 votes, and 7 others each to Mr. Adams and Mr. Pinckney. The 10 electors of Maryland divided equally between Jefferson and Burr, and also equally between Adams and Pinckney. The North Carolina electors were similarly divided.

The 12th amendment of the Constitution was an outcome of that memorable contest, requiring the electors to vote separately for President and Vice President. Under that amendment only one election took place, prior to Van Buren, in which the electors of one or more States were not divided in their choice according to personal preferences, as the following memoranda will show:

Fifth election (1804). Of the 11 electors of Maryland, 9 voted for Jefferson and 2 for C. C. Pinckney.

Sixth election (1808). Of the 19 electors of New York, 13 voted for Madison and 6 for George Clinton. Of the 11 of Maryland, 9 voted for Madison and 2 for C. C. Pinckney. Of the 14 of North Carolina, 11 voted for Madison and 3 for Pinckney.

Seventh election (1812). Of the 11 electors of Maryland, 6 voted for Madison and 5 for DeWitt Clinton.

Eighth election (1816). In this election none of the colleges were divided for President, though for Vice President Connecticut was divided between James Ross and John Marshall. The candidates for President were James Monroe and Rufus King.

Ninth election (1820). Of the 8 electors of New Hampshire, 7 voted for Monroe and 1 for John Q. Adams. Excepting this one, Monroe received the votes of all the electors appointed. For Vice President, three of the colleges were divided.

Tenth election (1824). Of the 36 electors of New York, 1 voted for Jackson, 26 for J. Q. Adams, 5 for W. H. Crawford, and 4

	Population		Minors	
	M	F	M	F
Lybrand, Geo. C., res Lybrand block, e Front st.	1			
Lyman, William, machinist, res Sugar & Norton.	1	1		
Lyman, John, laborer, res n Norton street. -	3	1	2	
Lyman, James Thomas, laborer, res n Norton st.	1			
Lynch, Rev. Sam'l, Life Ins. Agt., res n West st.	1	2		
Lynch, Miss Ida, res n West street.				
Lynch, Samuel, Jr., tel'g. operator, res n West st.	1			
LYAL, JOHN, County Commissioner, res near Centerbugh.				
Lybarger, Mrs. Mary, res w Vine street. - -	1	1	1	
Lybarger, Ella, hair dresser, res w Vine street. -		1		

M

	Population		Minors	
	M	F	M	F
Magers, Susan, res cor Chestnut & Mechanic sts. -		1		
Magers, Florence, milliner, s Main, res e Gambier		1		
Magers, Calvin, city marshal, res e Burgess st. -	3	3	2	2
Magers, Nathan, farmer, res Sandusky street. -	1	2		
Magill, John, shoemaker, w High, res w Gambier	3	4	2	3
Magill, Robert, brick mason, res e Chestnut st. -	1	2		1
MACKEY, HENRY A., Agent C. Mt. V. & C. R.R., res cor Vine and Gay sts. - - -	1	2		1
Mackey, Samuel A., traveling agent, residence w Hamtramck street. - - - - -	2	3		1
Mackey, John B., carpenter, res w Hamtramck.	1			
Mackey, Anna, music teacher, " "		1		
Martin, A. T., carpenter, 35 w High street. -	1	1		
Martin, John W., teamster, res Gay & Burgess. -	1	1		
Martin, David, carpenter, res n Gay street. -	2	2	1	1
Martin, Catharine, " " " -				
Martin, William, carpenter, " " -	1			
Martin, Warner, " . " " -	1			
MARTIN, JOSEPH S., cabinet maker, residence near foot of Main street. -	1	3		
Martin, Mary, res near foot Main street.				
Martin, Caroline, res " " "				
Martin, Ella, portrait painter, res near foot Main.				
Martin, J. P. R., clerk, residence " " "	1			
MARTIN, SAMUEL S., wagon maker, residence cor Front & Main street. - -	2	4	1	2
Martin, Fanny, res cor Front & Main street.				
Martin, Cora, " " " "				
Martin, Samuel, laborer, res n Catharine street. -	3	2	2	1
Martin, Geo. R., steam saw mill, Granville road.				
Martin, Harry, student, res " "				
Martin, R., saddler, res e Chestnut street. - -	2	1	1	
Martin, Mrs. Martha, res e Front. " - -		1		

for H. Clay. Of the 3 of Delaware, 1 voted for Adams and 2 for Crawford. Of the 11 of Maryland, 7 voted for Jackson, 3 for Adams, and 1 for Crawford. Of the 5 of Louisiana, 3 voted for Jackson and 2 for Adams. Of the 3 of Illinois, 2 voted for Jackson and 1 for Adams. The votes for Vice President were similarly given according to the preferences of the electors.

Eleventh election (1828). Of the 9 electors of Maine, 1 voted for Jackson and 8 for Adams. Of the 36 of New York, 20 voted for Jackson and 16 for Adams. Of the 11 of Maryland, 5 voted for Jackson and 6 for Adams. There were similar divisions for Vice President.

Twelfth election (1832). The college of Maryland was divided between Jackson and Clay. No divisions in electoral colleges since 1832 until 1872. The death of Horace Greeley left the electors chosen in his interest free. They voted as their preferences dictated.

OUR COAST LINES.

FEW persons not familiar with geography will believe that the Pacific ocean boundary of the United States has a greater extent of coast line than the Atlantic shore. The aggregate of our shore line on the Pacific is 12,734 miles, whilst on the Atlantic it is 11,860 miles, and on the Gulf of Mexico 6843 miles. California contains 1136 miles of the coast line on the Pacific, whilst she has also 272 miles of island shore and 240 miles of tide water river shore, making altogether 1648 miles of shore line. Texas has an actual coast line on the Gulf of 1279 miles, whilst Florida has 1144 miles on the Gulf, and 363 on the Atlantic, so that both exceed California in this particular. It is the annexation of Alaska that has promoted the Pacific coast to a higher figure than the Atlantic, Alaska having 9830 miles of coast line. These figures are from the Coast Survey Reports.

APPARENT AND MEAN TIME.

TIME is both apparent and mean. The sun is on the meridian at 12 o'clock on four days only in the year. It is sometimes as much as 16½ minutes before or after twelve when its shadow strikes the noon-mark on the sun-dial. This is occasioned by the irregular motion of the earth on its axis and the inclination of its poles. This is called apparent time. Mean time is determined by the equitation of these irregularities for every day in the year.

ANAXIMANDER, a philosopher, born at Miletus, Greece, B. C. 610, was the first to delineate the surface of the earth, and mark the divisions of land and water upon an artificial globe.

	Popu-lation.		Minors	
	M	F	M	F
Martin, Mrs. Ann, res e Front street. - - -		1		
Martin, Joseph, " " " - - -	1			
Martin, James, farmer, res Coshocton road.				
Martin, Alice, res Coshocton road.				
Martin, Pet, " " "				
Martin, Jessie, " " "				
Marple, A. C., farmer, res Morris township.				
Marshall, Mrs. Nancy, res Coshocton & Catharine	3		2	
Mayor's office, Council Chamber, n Gay street.				
Madden, Mrs. William, res e Chestnut street. -	2	3	2	2
March, Alexander, plasterer, res Oak street. -	4	4	3	2
MARSH, LYMAN W., Street Commissioner, res e Front street. - - - - - - -	1	3		2
MARSH, Prof. R. B., Supt. Union High School, res w Hamtramck street. - - - -	4	5	3	4
Marsh, A. William, student, res w Hamtramck.				
Marsh, Edward, farmer, " " -	1			
Mahaffey, William, brick maker, res Sandusky. -	6	1	5	
Mahaffey, Charles M., medical student, " -	1			
Mahaffey, James, blacksmith, res Prospect st. -	4	3	3	1
Mahaffey, Mrs. Letitia, res w High street. -		2		
Mahaffey, Elizabeth, " " " - -				
Mahaffey, Milton, blacksmith, res e Gambier st. -	3	2	2	1
Marken, Mrs. Ann, seamstress, " s Catharine st.		3		1
Maber, Mrs. Sarah, res e Front street. - -		1		
Mattison, Rev. T., " Mansfield avenue. - -	1	3		2
Masteller, Joseph, miller, res n Norton street. -	4	4	3	2
Masteller, Frank, boiler maker, " " -	2	1	1	
Marquand, Mrs. Eliza, res n Main street. - -		2		1
Maxwell, I. Douglas, machinist, res w High st. -	1	1		
Maxwell, William, laborer, res w Hamtramck st.	4	1	3	
MAWER, WILLIAM, Coal Dealer, residence corner Sugar and Norton streets. . - -	2	3	1	
Mawer, Hannah, res cor Sugar and Norton streets				
Mawer, Emma, " " "				
MAY, DANIEL W., pattern maker, residence e Vine street. - - - - - - -	4	1	3	
May, Clayton, carpenter, res e Vine street. - -	1			
Mead, Michael, laborer, " e Burgess street. -	3	4	2	3
Mead, Annie, teacher, res Mansfield avenue. -		1		
MEAD, D. W., dry goods merchant, s Main st. residence e Gambier street. - - - -	1	2		
Mead, Frank, clerk at D. W. Mead's, res e Gambier	1			
Mead, T. B., dry grocer, s Main, " " -	1			
Merriman, Waldo, medical student, res n Main.	1			
Merriman, —, law student, brds Mrs. Buckland's.	1			
Mefford, Mrs. Hannah, res w High street. - -		1		
Mefford, Jacob M., assessor 4th ward, res w High.	1			

	Popu-lation.		Minors	
Insure Yourselves and Property with **J. J. FULTZ, Agent.**	M	F	M	F
Metcalf, Nathaniel, laborer, res s Main street.	3	1	2	
Messenger, G. B., commercial traveler, res e High	2	2	1	1
Messenger, H. Clay, clerk, res e High street.	1			
Meeker, John, farmer, res e Vine street.	4	1	3	
Methodist Episcopal Church, s e corner Gay and Chestnut streets.				
Methodist (African) Church, s side Front st., near Mulberry street.				
Methodist Church, n Mulberry, near Sugar street.				
Methodist Parsonage, " " " "				
Merideth, John, stone cutter, res e Elizabeth st.	1	2		1
Mendenhall, E. I. M., attorney, res n Mulberry.	1	3		2
Miller, George, laborer, res w Vine street.	2	4	1	2
Miller, Wm. D., " " " "	1			
MILLER, EMMANUEL, grocer and grain merchant, w Gambier, res Mulberry & Gambier.	1	6		5
Miller, Mrs. Sarah, res Vine and Mulberry sts.		2		1
Miller, Jacob T., cooper, res cor Vine & Walnut.	3	2	2	1
Miller, Fred., works at oil mill, " "	1			
Miller, John T., clerk, " "	1			
Miller, Fred. D., cooper, res w Gambier street.	1	3		2
Miller, John, wood turner, " "	1			
MILLER, JAMES WARNER, dry goods merchant, s Main, res Vine and Gay streets.	1	4		1
Miller, Victoria, " " " "				
Miller, Jennie, " " " "				
Miller, Sue, " " " "				
Miller, Warner W., clerk, res e Front street.	1	2		
Miller, John, cooper, res w High street.	1	1		
Miller, Frank W.,merchant, s Main,res n Norton	1	2		1
Miller, Joseph, dealer in flour, corn, mill feed, &c. w Gambier, brds C. Peterman's, e Gambier.	1			
MILLER, ROBERT, ex-County Treasurer, res Pleasant township.				
Miller, Miss Roberta, res Pleasant township.				
Miller, William, " " "				
Miller, Miss Mary, " " "				
Milless, J. H. & Co., Clothiers, Kirk Hall s Main.				
MILLESS, J. H., (of the above firm,) residence w High street.	2	8	1	7
Mills, Richard, laborer, res Sandusky street.	3	3	2	2
Mills, M. L. & Co., dealers in Coal & Coke, s Main				
MILLS, M. L., (of the above firm,) township clerk, cor Main & Gambier sts., res s Gay st.	1	2		
Mill, Jonathan, carpenter, res e Vine street.	5	2	4	1
Mitchell, Mrs. M. H., brds at Rev. W. Thompson's e Chestnut.		2		
Mitchell, Mary, brds at Rev. Thompson's, Chestnut				

Insure Yourselves in the C. M. L. & H. I. Co., of Mt. Vernon, O.	Population.		Minors	
	M	F	M	F
MITCHELL, D. S., Family Grocer, e side of Public Square, res e Chestnut street. - -	4	1	3	
Mitchell, Albert, brick mason, res e Front street.	1	2		
Mitchell, Mary, res e Front street.				
Mitchell, John A., brick mason, res e Front st. -	3	3	2	2
MITCHELL, SILAS, farmer, residence west High street. - - - - - -	1	2		
Mitchell, Mrs. Ann, res w High street. -		2		
Mitchell, Mrs. Lydia, res Chestnut & Jefferson. -		1		
Mitchell, William, Iron Fence Manufacturer, res Jefferson and High streets. - - -	2	2	1	1
Mitchell, Capt. L. Y., clerk, res Jefferson & High	1			
Mitchell, Q. A., clerk with D. W. Mead, s Main, res Hamtramck & Mulberry streets. -	1	2		1
Mitchell, R. C., clothier, n Main, res e Lamartin.	2	3	1	1
Mitchell, Edger, grocer, res e Plimpton street. -	1	4		2
Montanya, Alonzo, laborer, res e Burgess street.	2	3	1	2
Montanya, John, cooper, res w Gambier street. -	2	1	1	
Moore, William, boiler maker, res n Gay street -	1	2		1
MOORE, JOHN, " " north Mulberry street. - - - - - - -	5	1		
Moore, William B., boiler maker, res n Mulberry.	2	1	1	
Moore, William, pattern maker, res Sandusky st.	4	2	3	
MOORE, FRANK R., attorney, with Col. W. C. Cooper, s Main, res Sandusky street. -	1			
Moore, A. C., baker, shop and res e Gambier st.	3	5	2	4
Moore, A. B., supt. woolen mill, res w Vine st. -	2	3	1	2
MONTGOMERY, D. C., attorney, north-west side Public Square, res Main & Hamtramck.	1	2		1
Montis, William M., clerk, res w High street.	1			
Montis, Solomon, farmer, res Boynton street. -	3	1	2	
Monahan, Thomas, laborer, res Coshocton ave. -	3	8	2	7
Monahan, Daniel, painter, " " " -	1			
Monahan, Daniel, Sr., laborer, res e High street.	1	2		1
Monahan, Daniel, Jr., moulder, " e "	1			
Monroe, W. T., "Great Western," res w Vine st.	3	2	2	1
Monroe, Belle, res w Vine street.				
Morrow, Nathan, res e Chestnut street. - -	2	2	1	1
MORGAN, GEN. G. W., Attorney, Kirk Hall, res cor Gambier and McKenzie streets.	1	4		1
Morgan, Miss Kate, res Gambier & McKenzie sts.				
Morgan, William, farmer, res Pleasant township.				
Morris, David, carpenter, res w Chestnut street. -	1	1		
Mount Vernon Iron Works, (C. & G. Cooper & Co. proprietors,) cor Sugar & Sandusky streets.				
MOUNT VERNON REPUBLICAN, office No. 5, Kremlin building, Public Square.				
Mount Vernon Gas Light and Coke Co.'s works foot of Mulberry street.				

Insure against Fire and Lightning. *J. J. Fultz, Agt.*	Popu-lation.		Minors	
	M	F	M	F

MOUNT VERNON DEMOCRATIC BANNER, office cor Main and Gambier streets.

Mount Vernon Soap Manufactory, works "Owl's Head," near Fair Grounds.

Mount, Sylvia, teacher, res w High street.   - | | 1 | |

Muenscher, Rev. Joseph, Episcopal Clergyman, residence e High street.   -   -   - | 1 | 1 |

MULVANY, OSCAR M., machinist, residence w Sugar street.   -   -   -   - | 2 | 1 | 1 |

Mulvany, James R., res w Sugar street.

Muldowney, Edward, laborer, res Railroad street. | 1 | 4 | | 3

Mulhearn, Bryan, Engr. C. Mt. V. & C. R. R., res cor Vine and Mulberry streets.   -   - | 1 | |

Mumaw, John, carpenter, res Sandusky street. | 1 | 1 |

Murphy, Mrs. Dennis, res s Gay street.   -   - | 1 | 4 | 1 |

Murphy, Rose,   "   "   "

Murphy, Minnie,   "   "   "

Murphy, M. M., "General Jobber," res n Main. | 1 | 1 |

Murphy's, Mrs., Ice Cream Rooms, near cor Main street and Public Square.

Murphy, Mrs. Samuel, res e Water street.   -   - | | 2 |

Murphy, Patrick, laborer, res w High street.   - | 3 | 5 | 2 | 3

Murphy, Marshall N., tinner, cor Mulberry and High streets, res n Jefferson street.   - | 2 | 2 | 1 | 1

Murphy, Oliver F., clerk, Knox Mu. Ins. Co., res w High street.   -   -   -   - | 2 | 2 | 1 | 1

Murphy, Dello, laborer, res w High street.   - | 1 | |

Murphy, Thos. L., farmer, res w High street. | 1 | 1 |

Murphy, John, moulder, res cor Vine & Rogers. | 3 | 1 | 2 |

Murray, Patrick,   "   "   Sandusky street. | 5 | 6 | 4 | 4

MYERS, JOHN, County Recorder, Court House, res cor Front and McArthur streets.   -   - | 1 | 4 | | 3

Myers, Mrs. Elinor, res Catharine & Gambier sts. | | 2 |

Myers, Jacob B., farmer, res e Gambier streets.   - | 1 | 1 |

Myers, Max, "Second Hand Emporium," corner Gambier and Walnut, residence same.   - | 4 | 2 | 3 | 1

Mc

McArdle, Dennis, laborer, res w Vine street.   - | 1 | 1 |

McBride, T. & Son, proprietors Bergin House cor Main and Front streets.

McBRIDE, THOMAS, (of the above firm,) residence Bergin House.   -   -   -   - | 1 | 2 |

McBride, Ellen, boards at Bergin House.

McBRIDE, THOMAS J., (of the firm of T. McBride & Son,) res Bergin House.   -   - | 1 | 2 | | 1

	Population M | F		Minors M | F	

	M	F	M	F
McCARTHY, DANIEL, moulder, residence w High street.	2	4	1	2
McCreary, Thomas, lumberman, res s Norton st.	1	1		
McCreary & Sanderson, lumber dealers, yard cor High & Sandusky streets.				
McCreary, Robert B., (of the above firm,) res w High street.	1	2		1
McCreary, Mrs. Mary, res n Gay street.		2		
McCracken, William, plasterer, res w High street	1			
McClurgin, Fanny, res s Mulberry street.		1		
McCombs, Solomon, teamster, res w High street.	1	2		
McCombs, William R., " " " "	1			
McCombs, Mrs. Belle, res Thistle Ridge.	1	1	1	
McCormick, Willis & Banning, furniture manufacturers, works w Vine, store room, s Main				
McCormick, Joseph, (of the above firm,) res cor Mulberry and Sugar streets.	4	6	3	4
McChristol, O., laborer, res cor Monroe & Chester	1	2		1
McClelland, D.T., clerk at T.B.Mead's, res e Front	1	2		1
McClelland & Culbertson, attorneys, e High street				
McCLELLAND, WILLIAM, (of the above firm,) res e High street.	1			
McClelland, Esther, res e High street.		1		
McClelland, Walter, farmer, res Danville road.				
McConnell & Boyd, dealers in glass ware, tin ware and notions, &c., cor Gay and Gambier sts.				
McConnell, J. S., (of the above firm,) res s Gay.	1	1		
McCulloch, William, laborer, res n Main street.	1	3		3
McCulloch, James, " " n Gay "	1	3		2
McCulloch, Andrew, moulder, res Cemetery ave.	1	1		
McCulloch, Mrs. Eliza, res Cemetery avenue.	1	3	1	2
McDowell, Daniel, cabinet maker, res w Vine st.	1	2		
McDowell, John, Undertaker, Woodward Hall, res w Vine street.	1			
McDowell, Dan., wood turner, res w Vine street.	1			
McDaniels, William, laborer, " "	3	2	2	1
McDough, James, " " "	2	4	1	2
McElroy, Mrs. Thomas, res e Chestnut street.		3		2
McElroy, Mrs. Ebenezer, " "		1		
McElroy, John, farmer, res Monroe township.				
McFeeley, W. J., Ins. Agt., Kirk Hall, boards at Bergin House.	1			
McFarland, Mrs. James, res Newark road.				
McFarland, J. H. & Co., dealers in hardware, nails, glass, &c., s Main, below Gambier st.				
McFARLAND, J. H., (of the above firm,) res e Gambier street.	1	2		
McFarland, Miss E. May, res e Gambier street.				

14

Every large Business Man in the City of New York has his life Insured. Call on J. J. Fultz, Agt.	Population.		Minors	
	M	F	M	F
McFarland, W. Z., (of the firm of J. H. McFarland & Co.,) residence e Gambier street.	2	1	1	
McFarland, Ira M., farmer, res Morgan tp.				
McFarland, Geo. W., sewing machine agent, res corner Front & McArthur streets.	2	3	1	1
McFarland, Clara, res corner Front & McArthur.				
McFadden, Samuel, boot and shoe dealer, s Main, near Gambier, res e High street.	2	2	1	1
McFadden, John, plasterer, res w Vine street.	3	3	2	1
McGibony, James, farmer, res Wooster avenue.	1	2		1
McGibony, John, " " Wooster road.				
McGiffin, N., res corner West & Chestnut streets.	1	2		1
McGrady, Daniel, shoemaker, res n Mulberry st.	1			
McGuire, John, res w High street.	1			
McGaughey, Mrs. William, res e High near Gay.	1	2	1	1
McIntire & Kirk, attorneys, Judge Hurd's office, n Main, near Chestnut street.				
McIntire, A. R., (of the above firm,) res e High.	3	2	2	2
McKane, Arch'd., shoemaker, res s Mulberry st.	3	3	2	2
McKay, Erick, brick mason, res e Chestnut st.	1	2		
McKay, W. W., stone mason, res Pleasant tp.				
McKee, Thos., paper and rag dealer, res corner of Norton and Gambier streets.	1	5		4
McKee, Matthew, peddler, res w Gambier street.	3	3	2	2
McKENNA, J. B., marble dealer, north-west side Public Square, res w Vine street.	2	3	1	2
McKown, G. E., dentist, cor Main & Vine, res e Gambier street.	4	4	3	3
McKown, Jennie res e Gambier street.				
McKibbon, Joseph, res cor High and West sts.	1	4		
McMann, D. C., chief cook, Rowley House.	1			
McManis, Susan, help, Rowley House.		1		
McMillen & Russell, physicians and surgeons, w side Main, btw Pub. Sqr. and Chestnut.				
McMillen, John, (of the above firm,) brds at Mrs. Buckland's.	1	1		
McMillen, Anabel, teacher, brds Mrs. Buckland's		1		
McMullen, Mrs. Margaret, res w Gambier street.		2		
McMullen, Ellen, " " "				
McMULLEN, DANIEL, railroad contractor, res w Gambier street.	1			
McNeil, Nathaniel, laborer, res e High street.	2	1	1	
McPherson, Charles, [c] " " e " "	1			
McVicker, Mrs. Lucinda, res Mulberry & Vine.		1		
McVicker, Thomas, laborer, " "	1			
McWherter, Rev. G. W., res "Orphan's Home," Gambier road.				

NEW GROCERY

—AND—

PROVISION STORE.

Arthur E. Philo

RESPECTFULLY announces to the citizens of *MOUNT VERNON* and *VICINITY*, that he has opened a

NEW GROCERY & PROVISION STORE

in GEORGE'S BLOCK, Main Street, opposite Baker Bros' Drug Store, where will be found a

Large, Fresh and well Selected Stock of

FAMILY GROCERIES,

—AND—

CONFECTIONERIES.

☞ CASH PAID FOR COUNTRY PRODUCE. ☜

OYSTERS.

FRESH CAN & TUB OYSTERS,

Received Daily during the Season.

CALL AND SEE ME.

Every Farmer, Mechanic, and Laborer, should have his Life insured. J. J. Fultz *represents Standard Companies.*	Popu-lation.		Minors	
	M	F	M	F

N

Neiser, Joseph, brewer, res w Vine street. - -	5	3	4	2
Newby, James, tailor, n Main, res e Sugar street.	1	5		1
Newby & Shenan, milliners, s Main street.				
Newby, Julia, (of the above firm,) res e Sugar st.				
Newby, Margaret, res e Sugar street.				
Newby, Ellen, " "				
Newby, Therese, " "				
New, John, machinist, res n Gay street. - -	1	1		
New, James, laborer, res Railroad street. - -	1			
Newton, Rev. O. H., Pastor Presbyterian Church, res e High street. - - - -	4	3	3	2
Newman, Milton, [c] laborer, res e Vine street. -	2	5	1	4
Neal, Geo. D., carriage maker, w Front, res e Vine	1	2		1
Nichols, Mrs. Mary, res cor Mulberry & Front sts		2		
Nichols, F. C., sewing machine agent, res corner Harrison and Chestnut streets. - - -	1	2		1
Nixon, Daniel S., farmer, res e Chestnut street. -	2	2	1	1
Norton & Kindricks, milliners, s Main street.				
Norton, Mrs. Jane, (of the above firm,) residence corner Mulberry and Sugar streets. - -		2		
Norton, Julia, res " "				
Norton, William B., clerk, res Mulberry & Sugar.	1			
Norton, Geo. K., grocer, n Main, res corner High and Norton streets. - - - -	2	3	1	
Norton, Mrs. A. Baldwin, brds at J. Sapp's, s Gay	1	1	1	
Norton, A. Baldwin, student, brds " "				
Noth, Charles, shoemaker, res e Hamtramck st.	1			

O

Odbert, Thomas, wool buyer, res w Chestnut st. -	1	1		
Odbert, Thomas H., res w Chestnut street. -	1			
Oglevie, Mrs. Hugh, " e Gambier street. - -		2		1
Oram, James E., carpenter, res e Plimpton street.	1	2		1
Osborne, Mrs. Susan, res w Vine street. - -		1		
Osborne, W. J. S., carpenter, res e High street. -	2	3	1	2
Osborne, Miss M. C., " "				
OSBORNE, CHARLES H., baggage master B. & O. R.R., res w High street. - - -	4	2	3	1
O'Brien, Andrew, laborer, res w Gambier street.	2	2	1	1
O'BOYLE, CORNELIUS, machinist, residence e Plimpton street. - - - -	2	2	1	1
O'Boyle, John, machinist, res Harkness road.				
O'Conner, Bridget, res e Gambier street. - -		1		

	Population.		Minors	
Insure Yourselves in the C. M. L. & H. I. Co., of Mt. Vernon, O.	M	F	M	F
O'Hara, Mary, brds with Geo. Winne, e Chestnut.		1		
O'Rourke, O., laborer, res Mansfield avenue. -	2	4	1	2
O'Rourke, Charles, tinner, " " -	1			
O'Rourke, Thomas, tailor, " " -	1			
P				
Parish, Garrett, commercial traveler, res e Curtis.	2	5	1	4
Parr, Silas, boot maker, w High, res e Sugar st. -	1	3		2
Parr, Henry, stone cutter, " " -	1			
Paazig, Mrs. Margaret J., res Sandusky street. -		1		
Paazig, Max, carpenter, " Vine & McKenzie.	4	1	3	
Parker, David, res s Mechanic street. - - -	5	2	4	1
Parker, H. C., res w Gambier, brds Rowley House	1	1		
Parker, Mrs. Fanny, [H. C.] milliner, s Main st.				
Park, Mrs. Elizabeth, res e Gambier street. - -		2		
Parrott, Arthur, farmer, res Newark road.				
Parrott, David, " "				
Parrott, Andrew, " Granville road.				
Parrott, William, " Utica "				
Parke, D. W., deputy clerk Court Common Pleas, res Mansfield avenue. - - - -	1			
Parke, T. V., Sr., Justice Peace, No. 2, Kremlin, res Mansfield avenue. - - - -	1	2		
Parke, Kate, " "				
Parke, T. V., Jr., clerk, res Mansfield avenue. -	1			
Parks, Thomas, boot maker, Pub. Sqr., res n Main	3	3	2	2
Park, Joseph, farmer, res Pleasant township.				
Park's Floral Gazette, No. 1, Kremlin, Pub. Sqr.				
Park, Geo., edr. Floral Gazette, res Vine & Norton	1	2		1
Paige, Creighton, marble cutter, res e Vine street.	1	1		
Page, Mrs. James, res Wooster avenue. - -		1		
Patterson & Alsdorf, dealers in lumber, yard cor West & Gambier sts., near B. & O. R. R.				
PATTERSON, JAMES, (of the above firm,) res corner West and Chestnut streets. - - -	3	2	2	1
Patterson, Elwin Linn, res West & Chestnut sts.				
Patterson, Dora, " " "				
Patterson, Mrs. ——, " " "		1		
Patton, W. T., boot & shoe dealer, Banning Hall, w Vine st., brds at James Sapp's, s Gay st.	1			
Patton, Mrs. Elizabeth, brds " " " -		1		
Payne, Raphael, painter, res e High street. -	2	3	1	1
Payne, John, clerk, " " " -	1			
Payne, Rev. Henry, Episcopal Clergyman, residence cor Chestnut and Mulberry streets. -	4	1	3	1
Payne, Miss Jane, physician, office, N. N. Hill's block, res cor Chestnut and Mulberry sts. -		1		

Every Young Business Man should have his Life insured. Fultz. Agt.

	Popu-lation.		Minors	
	M	F	M	F
PAYNE, JOHN, miller, res Madison street. -	1	4		
Payne's, Misses, milliners and vest makers, east Vine street, opposite Post Office.				
Payne, R. N., of the above, res Madison street.				
Payne, L. E., " " " "				
Payne, Mary, " " " "				
Payne, John R., miller, " " " -	1			
Payne, E. T., boiler maker, " " " -	1	2		1
Paul, Jacob, eng. Cooper's foundry, res n Norton.	1	2		1
Palmer, Josiah, res e Sugar street. - - -	1	3		
Palmer, Alice, " " "				
Palmer, Celia, " " "				
Peugh, Frank, porter at Rowley House. - -	1			
Peugh, Henry H., tanner, res w Gambier street.	4	2	3	1
Peugh, Mrs. A., res cor Norton & Burgess street.		1		
Peugh, George W., moulder, " " " -	1			
Pearl, Peter, laborer, res n Gay street. - -	1			
Peardon, John, teamster, res e Elizabeth street. -	1	1		
Pelton, Mark, pattern maker, res Sandusky st. -	2	2	1	1
Penick & Ransom, butchers, Jones' block, w High				
Penick, William, (of the above firm,) res "	1	2		1
Penick, J. C., clerk, res w High street.	1			
Peoples, William, dairy man, res w Sugar street.	2	3	1	2
Pepper, Rev. G. W., pastor Methodist Episcopal Church, res w Chestnut street. - - -	2	3	1	2
Pepper, Charles M., student, res w Chestnut st.				
Pepper, Samuel A., " "	1			
Pepper, Miss Lena,		1		
Perings, Mrs. L., laundress at Rowley House. -		1		
Peterman, C., & Son, dry goods merchants, corner Main and Gambier streets.				
PETERMAN, C., (of the above firm,) residence corner Gambier and McKenzie streets. -	2	3	1	1
Peterman, Charles P., student, Kenyon College, res cor McKenzie and Gambier streets.				
Peterman, Miss Emma, res McKenzie & Gambier				
Peterman, " Lu, " " "				
PETERMAN, S. H., (of the firm of Peterman & Son,) res McKenzie and Gambier streets. -	1			
Phenice, Abram, carpenter, res Coshocton ave. -	1	3		2
Phifer, M. G., laborer, res e Chestnut street. -	1	1		
Phifer, Mrs. James, " n West street. - -		1		
Phifer, Prindle, carpenter, res n Gay street. - -	1	3		2
Phillips, Mrs. Henry, res w High street. - -		1		
PHILLIPS, IRA M., butcher, s Main, near cor Main and Gambier, res e High street. - -	1	2		1

Insure Yourselves and Property with *J. J. FULTZ, Agent.*	Popu- lation.		Minors	
	M	F	M	F
Philo, George, farmer, res Mansfield and Fredericktown road.				
PHILO, ARTHUR E., Family Grocer, s Main, near Gambier, res same building. - - -	1	3		2
Pickard, William, farmer, res cor Gay & Curtis. -	4	4	3	3
Pickard, Belle, " " "				
PICKARD, PETER, physician, n Main, near Chestnut, res w High street. - - -	3	3	2	2
Pickering, J. S., jeweler, res High & McArthur.	1			
Pierce, Mrs. William M., res e Vine street. -	1	1	1	
Pike, Abram, brick maker, res e Hamtramck st.	1			
Pike, Mrs. Mary, " " " -		1		
Place, James, cooper, res w Gambier street. -	3	1	2	
Plank, J. O., Day Clerk, at Rowley House. -	1		1	
Plimpton, Mrs. Elizabeth, res Main & Sugar. -	2	3	2	
Plimpton, Elizabeth H., " " "		1		
Pollock, Mrs. Mary, res Mansfield avenue.		1		
PONTING, JOHN, Grocer and County Commissioner, s e corner Main & Gambier, residence e Gambier street. - - - - - -	1			
PORTER, HENRY T., attorney for B. & O RR, res cor High and Ridgely streets, - - -	3	2	2	2
Porter, Ella, residence cor High and Ridgely.				
Porter, William H., " " "				
Porter, Walter H., " " "				
Porter, Mrs. America, res Sandusky street. -	1	2	1	1
Porter, B. J., carpenter, res s Norton " -	2	1	1	
Porter, Mrs. W. R., res e Vine street. - -	1	1	1	
Potter, Mrs Ellen, " e High " - -		1		
Potwin, Mrs. George B., res e Gambier street. -		1		
POWER, JOHN B., butcher, w Vine, residence w Vine street. - - - - - -	5	2	4	1
Power, John, miller, res e Burgess street. - -	1	3		
Power Melvilla C., " " " -				
Power, Martha A., " " " -				
Power, Samuel, butcher, " " -	1			
Power, J. W., miller, " " -	1			
Power, Thomas, " " " -	1			
Pratt, Miss Mary, residence w High street.		1		
Pratt, " Catharine, " " " -		1		
Presbyterian Church, n e cor Gay & Chestnut.				
Price, Harry, carpenter, res McKenzie & Water.	1	3		2
Price, Vesay, farmer, res Delaware road.				
Protestant Episcopal Church, cor High & Gay sts.				
" " Parsonage, n side e Chestnut				
Prosecuting Attorney's office, s side Chestnut st., between Gay and McKenzie streets.				
Pumphrey, W. B., physician, s side e Gambier, near Main, res Newark road.				

Every Farmer, Mechanic, and Laborer, should have his Property insured. J. J. Fultz represents Standard Companies.	Population.		Minors	
	M	F	M	F
Purcell, John, drayman, res Coshocton avenue. -	4	4	3	3
Purcell, Patrick, student, " " "				
Purcell, Michael, telg. operator, " "				
PYLE, C. S., clerk, Probate Court, & city clerk, res e High street. - - - -	2	3	1	2
Pyle, Ella F., res e High street.				
Pyle, Carrie C., " " "				
Pyle, Charles W., teller Savings Bank, res e High				
Pyle, Henry P., clerk, res cor Sugar & Gay sts. -	1			
Pyle, Mrs. Mary, res Cemetery avenue. - -		1		
Pyle, Parker B., tailor, cor Gambier & Main sts.. res e Gambier street. - - - -	2	3	1	1
Pyle, Mary, res e Gambier street.				
Pyle, E. W., teller Knox Co. National Bank, res e Gambier street.				

Q

Quaid, Dennis, salesman with M. Leopold, the Clothier, boards at the Bergin House. - -	1			
Quaid, David, laborer, res Sandusky street. - -	1			
Quaid, Mrs. Catharine, " " " - -		1		
Quaid, Mary Ann, " " " - -		1		
Quaid, Katie, " " " - -		1		1

R

Ralls, J. W., [c] tanner, res e Vine street. - -	3	7	2	4
Ralls, Thornton, [c] gardener, res w Vine street.	1			
Ralls, John, [c] laborer, res w Gambier street. -	1	2		1
Ransom, Henry, brick mason, res e Chestnut st. -	2	1	1	
Ransom, Oscar, " " " -	3	1	2	
Ransom, Abraham," " " e Vine street. -	1	2		1
Ransom & Penick, butchers, w High street.				
Ransom, John H., (of the above,) res w High st.	1	2		1
Rathell, Parrott, carpenter, res e Gambier street.	1			
Rathell, Mrs. S. M., boarding house, e Gambier.		1		
RAYMOND, G. E., city tannery, w Gambier, res cor High and Walnut streets. - - -	1	3		2
Raymond, Mrs. Elnathan, res w High streets. -		2		
Reeve, Miss Louisa, res cor Chestnut & Mechanic		1		
REEVE, JOHN Y., boot and shoemaker, cor Main and Front, res w Vine street. - -	2	4	1	2
Reeve, Miss Ella, Hair Dresser, e Vine, opposite post office, res w Vine street. - -				
Reeve, Amy, res w " "				

15

ROBERT WRIGHT. HENRY C. WRIGHT.

—— [o] ——

ROBERT WRIGHT & SON,

Builders & Contractors,

Gambier, Ohio,

RESPECTFULLY announces to the citizens of KNOX COUNTY that they are, at all times, ready to take

CONTRACTS

for erecting BUILDINGS of every description. Having the

MOST APPROVED MACHINERY,

THEY WILL FURNISH

DOORS, WINDOW SASH AND

WINDOW BLINDS,

as cheaply and as expediously as any other establishment in the county.

Persons contemplating to build, can, if they desire, examine specimens of our workmanship, which can be found all over Gambier. Our work is all warranted.

OUR WORK SPEAKS FOR ITSELF.

FURNITURE,

of every description, made to order, of the best materials, and at prices warranted to give satisfaction.

GIVE US A CALL,

examine our work, and obtain our prices, before contracting elsewhere.

UNDERTAKING,

A SPECIALTY.

	Popu-lation.		Minors	
The life of Horace Greeley was insured for one hundred thousand dollars. Call on J. J. Fultz, Agt.	M	F	M	F
Reese, Mrs., dress maker, e Vine, opposite post office, res w Gambier street. - - -		1		
REES, WILLIAM, baggage master, C. Mt. V. & C. R.R., Gann Accom., res e Front street.	2	1	1	
Redman, George S., laborer, res e High street. -	1			
Reedy, Philip, brick mason, res e Gambier st. -	1			
Reed, Mrs., Eliza, res s Mulberry street. - -		1		
Reed, Leander, " " " -	1			
Reed & Clements, sash manufacturers, n Sandusky				
Reed, Lewis, (of the above,) res w Gambier st. -	2	3	1	2
Reed, John, res cor Front and Mechanic streets. -	2	3	1	3
Reed, Mrs. Marg., brds with J. M. Styers, e Front		2		
Reed, Miss Olla, " " "				
Reynolds, Mrs. J. E., res e Chestnut street. -	1	2	1	1
Reynolds, Laura, " " "				
Reynolds, S. H., clerk, " " "				
Reynolds, James, laborer, res e Burgess street. -	2	5	1	4
Rector, Charles, laborer, res Railroad street. -	1	1		
Rector, Mrs. ——, res n Main street. - -		1		
Ringwalt & Jennings, dry goods merchants, cor Public Square and Main street.				
RINGWALT, JOHN S., (of the above firm,) res e Vine street. - - - - - -	3	4	2	1
Rinehart, John, engr. C. Mt. V. & C. R.R., res e Front street. - - - - - - -	4	2	3	1
Rinehart, Samuel, farmer, res Delaware road.				
Rinehart, Douglas, " " Clinton township.				
Richards, J. H., teacher, res e High street. -	1			
Roberts, Amos, blacksmith, res Sandusky street.	2	1	1	
Roberts, James, coal dealer, res Mulberry & Vine	1	4		3
Roberts, William, clerk, " " "	1			
Roberts, John H., carpenter, res Danville, O.				
Roberts, Milton, restaurant, s Main, res w Front.	2	1	1	
Roberts, Mrs. Eliza, seamstress, res n Gay street.		2		
Roberts, Miss ——, " " "				
ROBERTS, WID. P., restaurant, s Main, opposite Rowley House, res same building. - -	4	2	3	1
Roberts, Joseph, cabinet maker, res e Gambier. -	2	2	1	
Roberts, J. M., confectioner, s Main, res n Norton	1	1		
Robinson, Mrs. Nancy, res Vine & Jefferson sts. -		1		
Robinson, R. J. & W. S., physicians and surgeons, e Gambier, btw Main and Gay sts.				
Robinson, R. J., (of the above,) res e Gambier. -	1			
Robinson, W. S., (of the above,) " " -	1			
Robinson, Mrs. Rebecca, res e Chestnut street. -	1	1	1	
Robinson, L., physician, e Gambier, res e Chestnut	1	1		
Robinson, R. J., druggist, brds Rowley House. -	1			
Robinson, Basil, farmer, res near Columbus road.				

Presidents of the United States.

PRESIDENTS.	NATIVITY.	BORN.	DIED.	AGE.
George Washington,	Vir.	Feb. 22, 1732.	Dec. 14, 1799.	67
John Adams,	Mass.	Oct. 19, 1735.	July 4, 1826.	91
Thomas Jefferson,	Vir.	April 2, 1743.	July 4, 1826.	83
James Madison,	Vir.	Mar. 16, 1751.	June 28, 1836.	85
James Monroe,	Vir.	Aprl 28, 1758.	July 4, 1831.	73
John Quincy Adams,	Mass.	July 11, 1767.	Feb. 23, 1848.	81
Andrew Jackson,	S. C.	Mar. 18, 1767.	June 8, 1845.	78
Martin Van Buren,	N. Y.	Dec. 5, 1782.	July 24, 1862.	80
W. H. Harrison,	Vir.	Feb. 9, 1773.	April 4, 1841.	68
* John Tyler,	Vir.	Mar. 29, 1790.	Jan. 17, 1862.	72
James K. Polk,	N. C.	Nov. 2, 1795.	June 15, 1849.	54
Zachary Taylor,	Vir.	Nov. 24, 1784.	July 9, 1850.	66
† Millard Fillmore,	N. Y.	Jan. 7, 1800.	Mar. 8, 1874.	74
Franklin Pierce,	N. H.	Nov. 23, 1804.	Oct. 8, 1869.	65
James Buchanan,	Penn.	Aprl 13, 1791.	June 1, 1868.	77
Abraham Lincoln,	Ken.	Feb. 12, 1809.	April 15, 1865.	56
‡ Andrew Johnson,	N. C.	Dec. 29, 1808.	July 31, 1875.	67
Ulysses S. Grant,	Ohio.	Aprl 22, 1822.	Still living.	—

Ages of Presidents on Retiring from Office.

PRESIDENTS.	RETIRED.		SERVED.	AGE
George Washington,	Retired,	1797.	8 years.	65
John Adams,	"	1801.	4 years.	66
Thomas Jefferson,	"	1809.	8 years.	62
James Madison,	"	1817.	8 years.	58
James Monroe,	"	1825.	8 years.	59
John Quincy Adams,	"	1829.	4 years.	58
Andrew Jackson,	"	1837.	8 years.	62
Martin Van Buren,	"	1841.	4 years.	55
W. H. Harrison,	Died,	1841.	1 month.	68
John Tyler,	Retired,	1845.	3 years 11 mos.	55
James K. Polk,	"	1849.	4 years.	54
Zachary Taylor,	Died,	1850.	1 year 4 mos.	66
Millard Fillmore,	Retired,	1854.	2 years 8 mos.	53
Franklin Pierce,	"	1858.	4 years.	53
James Buchanan,	"	1861.	4 years.	70
Abraham Lincoln,	Assassinated,	1865.	4 years 1½ mos.	56
Andrew Johnson,	Retired,	1869.	3 yrs. 10½ mos.	61
Ulysses S. Grant,	"	1877.	8 years.	55

* John Tyler, Vice President, President on death of Harrison.
† Millard Fillmore, V. " " " " " Taylor.
‡ Andrew Johnson, " " " " " " Lincoln.

	Popu-lation.		Minors	
Insure Yourselves and Property with **J. J. FULTZ, Agent.**	M	F	M	F
ROGERS, JAMES, Grocer, Rogers' block, west Vine, near Main, res w Hamtramck street. -	2	2	1	
Rogers, William Julius, res " "				
ROGERS, EDWARD, meat market, Rogers' block, w Vine, resides in Gambier, O.				
Rogers, Timothy, machinist, res n Mulberry st. -	3	2	2	1
Rogers, Jennie, milliner, s Main, res n Mulberry.				
Rogers, Miss Belle, res cor Pub. Sqr. & High st. -		1		
Rogers, " Maggie, " " -		1		
ROGERS, Gen. GEORGE, (of the firm of C. & G. Cooper & Co.,) res cor Gambier & Division	1	6		3
Rogers & Adams, Iron Store, e side Pub. Square.				
Rogers (James) & Brent, (S. J.,) City Flouring Mills, Grain Warehouse, and Woolen Factory, Norton's old stand.				
Rogers, John S., clerk, brds Rowley House. -	1	1		
Rogers, Mrs. Jos. D., res cor Chestnut & Sandusky	1	2	1	
Rose, Albert, restaurant, (of the firm of Cotton & Rose,) res e Water street. - - -	2	1	1	
Rose, Charles, laborer, res e Front street. -	1	1		
Rose, Orra, " " e Chestnut street. -	1	1		
Rose, William A., machinist, res Columbus road.				
Roupe, Jacob, farmer, res Sandusky street. - -	1	1		
Rouse, E. S. S., res e High street. - - -	1	1		
Rowe, Mrs. J. M., brds with R. Thompson, east Gambier street. - - - -		2		1
Rowley, Jerome, res corner Gay & Gambier sts. -	1	3		1
Rowley, Miss Maria L., " "				
Rowley House, near corner Main & Front streets.				
ROWLEY, H. YOUNG, proprietor Rowley House, boards Rowley House. - - -	1	2		1
Rowley, Horace, harness maker, s Main, res east Plimpton street. - - - - -	1	2		1
RUE, GEORGE W., Day Operator, B. & O. Depot, boards cor Vine & Jefferson streets. -	1		1	
Runyan, Mrs. William H., res e Burgess street. -		3		2
Runyan, A. G., res n Mulberry street. - - -	1			
Rush, Mrs. Job, res e High street. - - -		2		
Russell, Thomas, moulder, res n Norton street. -	2	2	1	1
Russell, Mrs. J. W., res w Wooster street. -	2	4	2	2
Russell & McMillen, Physicians & Surgeons, north Main, w side, near Public Square.				
RUSSELL, J. W., Sr., (of the above firm,) res e Gambier street. - - - - - -	1	3		1
Russell, Mary, res e Gambier street.				
RUSSELL, WILLIAM B., Druggist, s Main, w side, btw Vine & Gambier, res e Gambier st.	2	2	1	
Russell, William S., postal clerk, " " -	2	1	1	

	Popu-lation.		Minors	
Every Young Business Man should have his Life and Property insured. J. J. Fultz. Agt.	M	F	M	F
Russell, James, moulder, res Chestnut & Jefferson	2	4	1	3
Rumsey, J. W., contractor, res e Front street. -	1	1		
RUMSEY, O. DOUGLAS, carpenter, residence e Front street. - - - - - -	1			
Rutter, Elias, res s Main street. - - - -	2	3	1	2
Ryan, John, farmer, res Pleasant township.				

S

Sacks, Charles, blacksmith, res s Harrison street.	1	3		2
Sanderson & Dettra, livery and feed stable, west Front street, near Bergin House.				
Sanderson, W. H., (of the above,) res w Front st.	2	1	1	
Sanderson, Miss L., boards Rowley House. - -		1		
Sanderson & McCreary, lumber dealers, yard cor High and Sandusky streets.				
Sanderson, William, Sr., (of the above firm,) res corner Jefferson and High streets. - -	1	3		
SANDERSON, WILLIAM, Jr., livery & feed stable, w Vine, res cor Vine & Mulberry sts.	3	4	2	3
Sanderson, Chas. W., livery, res Vine & " -	1			
Sanderson, David, carriage maker, East street, res cor Water and East streets. - - - -	2	1	1	
Sanderson, Samuel, carriage painter, res s Gay st.	2	2	1	
Sanderson, Miss Eva, res s Gay street.				
Sandford, G. W., clerk with J. Ponting, res east Gambier street. - - - - - -	1	2		1
Sanford, Mrs. ——, res e High street. - -		2		1
Sanders, Mrs. Ellen, res Vine & Mulberry streets.		1		
Saunders, Lizzie, help at Rowley House. - -		1		
Saunders, Edward, moulder, res n Norton street.	3	2	2	1
Saunders, Walter, laborer, Chester & Washington	3	3	2	1
Saulsberry, Thomas, machinist, res Railroad st.	1	1		
SAPP, JAMES, boarding house, e side s Gay, between High and Vine streets. - - -	4	4	3	1
Sapp, Madison N., grocer, Pub. Sqr., e Chestnut.	3	3	2	2
Sapp, Jeff. C., dealer in agrl. implt., res e " -	2	3	1	2
Sapp, Mary, res e Chestnut street.				
Sapp, Jennie, " e " "				
Sapp, Mrs. Maj. W. R., res e High street. - -	1	2	1	
Sapp, W. R., Jr., " e " "				
Sapp, W. C., dry goods merchant, w side s Main, res cor Gay and Vine streets. - -	2	3	1	1
Sapp, Solomon, mail agent, B. & O. R. R., residence e Gambier street. - - - -	2	3	1	2
Schnebly, Mrs. Viola, res n Main street. - -		1		
Selman, Mr., patent right dealer, Central House.	1			

Insure Yourselves in the C. M. L. & H. I. Co., of Mt. Vernon, O.	Popu-lation.		Minors	
	M	F	M	F
Severns, David, plasterer, res w Chestnut street. -	2	2	1	
Severns, Anne belle, res w Chestnut street.				
Severns, William, carpenter, res Railroad street.	2	2	1	1
Severns, Walter, brick mason, res " "	1			
Severns, James, plasterer, res Chester street. -	2	4	1	3
Severns, Samuel, laborer, res Monroe street. -	2	2	1	1
Severns, Thomas, brick mason, " " - -	1			
Severns, Harrison, laborer, res Sandusky street. -	3	4	2	3
Severns, Jack, " " w Vine street.	3	3	2	2
Second Ward School House, n side w Gambier st.				
Selby, George, blacksmith, res s Mulberry street.	1			
Selegue, Matthias, sexton cemetery, res Prospect.	5	4	4	2
Selegue, Charles, barber, Woodward block, "				
SELEGUE, HENRY, Barber Shop and Bath Rooms, Woodward block, res Prospect street.	1			
Sellers, D. L., laborer, res w Sugar street. - -	4	4	3	3
Sellers, Chalmers, grocer, res w " " - -	1			
Sellers, John, ins. agent, res n Catharine street. -	1	3		2
SELLERS, JOHN, farmer—member of the constitutional convention of 1850, res Morgan tp				
Scalts, M. J., proprietor Scalts' Omnibus Line, w Front street, res e High street. - - -	2	2	1	
Scalts, Miss M. J., " e " "				
Scalts, M. E., 'Bus driver, res e High street.				
Secord, Walter, laborer, res n Catharine street. -	1			
Sedwell, George, res e Front street.	1			
Setzler, Valentine, machinist, res w Chestnut st.	2	2	1	1
SEMPLE, W. F., Dentist, Woodward Hall, cor Vine and Main, res w High street. - -	2	2	1	1
Seavolt, David, blacksmith, res Sandusky street.	4	3	3	2
Sensel, Luther, " " e Vine " -	1			
Sensel, Mrs. Catharine, dress maker, res e Vine.		4		1
Sensel, Lotta, " "				
Sensel, Ella, " "				
Scott, T. E., farmer, res Monroe township.				
Scott, Ann, teacher, " Wooster avenue.		3		
Scott, J. C., res Mansfield avenue. - -	1	2		
SCRIBNER, JOHN J., druggist and physician, near cor Main and Chestnut, res same. - -	3	1	2	
Sculley, Mrs. Joanna, res s Mechanic street. -	2	4	2	3
Seymour, E. T., pat. right agt., res w Pleasant st.	1			
Seymour, Mrs. S. J., res w Pleasant. - - -		5		
Seymour, Mary, " "				
Seymour, Emma, " "				
Seymour, Sade, " "				
Seymour, Florence, " "				
Silcott, William A., Insurance Agent, res e Vine.	1			
Silcott, Loudon, blacksmith, res e Vine street. -	1			

Every large Business Man in the City of New York has his Life and Property Insured. Call on J. J. Fultz, Agt.	Popu-lation.		Minors	
	M	F	M	F
Siler, Robert, student, res cor Gay and Gambier.	1		1	
Siler, Mrs. R. B., " " " -		3		2
Siler, Bessie, " " "				
Siler, Mary, " " "				
Shaffer, Arthur, butcher, at J.C.Irvine's, res e Front	1	1		
Shaw, Charles, carriage painter, res n Main st. -	2	2	1	1
Shaw, Mrs., seamstress, res e Chestnut st. -		1		
SHAW, WESLEY, clerk with Arthur E. Philo, s Main, res cor West and Hamtramck sts. -	1	1		
Shaw, John, woolen mfr., res West & Hamtramck	1	4		3
Shaw, Emma, " " "				
Shaw, Ella, " " "				
Shaw, Belle, " " "				
Sharpe, Mrs. Margaret, " n Mulberry street. -		2		1
Sharpe, Aaron, butcher, res e Chestnut street. -	3	2	2	1
Sharpe, Nelson, poney express, res Catharine st.	1	1		
Sharpnack, Elijah, res n Mulberry street. - -	1	2		2
Sharpnack, Mrs. Daniel, " " - -		1		
Sheriff's office, rear of the Court House.				
Sherwood, H., res e Gambier street. - -	1	2		
Sherr, Benjamin, laborer, res n Gay street. -	2	2	1	
Shehan, Michael, stone mason, res Sandusky st. -	3	3	2	1
Shehan & Newby, milliners, w side s Main street				
Shehan, Joanna, (of the above,) res Sandusky st.				
Shire, Mrs., res e Chestnut street. - - -		3		
Shinneberry, William, farmer, res Utica road.				
Shinneberry, E. B., farmer, res Granville road.				
Shrimplin & Lippitt, City Drug Store, w Vine st.				
Shrimplin, Mrs. Laura W., (of the above firm,) res e Chestnut street. - - - -		2		1
Shrimplin, Lewis, R. R. brakeman, res e Gambier	1			
Shira, Dr. George, coroner, res North Liberty.				
Shuman, Annie, help at Rowley House. - -	1			
Shuman, Maggie, " " " - -	1			
Shuman, Sadie, " " " - -	1			
Sites, James, [c] laborer, res Mulberry & Front. -	3	4	2	2
Simmons, Jonathan, [c] laborer, res e Vine st. -	5	2	4	1
Simons, H. J., res w Vine street. - - -	2	1	1	
Simpkins, Milton, teamster, res Sandusky street.	2	4	1	3
Skillen, George, painter, P. O. address Mt. Vernon				
Skeen, Washington, farmer, res Wooster road.				
Skeen, Alexander, res e High street. - -	1	2		1
Smale, Richard, laborer, res Sugar and Norton. -	1	2		1
Smale, Samuel, shoemaker, res e Chestnut street.	1	1		
Smale, Samuel S., teamster, res Monroe township				
Smith, Mrs. William H., res e High street. - -		3		
Smith, Ada, teacher, " " "				
Smith, Belle, " " "				

	Popu-lation.		Minors	
Every Farmer, Mechanic, and Laborer, should have his Property insured. J. J. Fultz represents Standard Companies.	M	F	M	F
Smith, George, shoemaker, res e Gambier street.	1			
Smith, Mrs. Sarah, res s Mulberry street. - -	1	1	1	
Smith, Mrs. Harvey W., res Chestnut & Mulberry		4		3
Smith, Kitty, " " "				
Smith, Mrs. William L., " w High street. -		3		1
Smith, Charles G., farmer, res w High street. -	2	1	1	
Smith, William, carpenter, res w High " -	5	4	4	3
Smith, Samuel, " " " " -	1			
Smith, Jerry, [c] barber, res w Vine " -	3	3	2	2
Smith, Albert, plasterer, res w High " -	1			
Smith, Henry C., carpenter, res n Mulberry st. -	1	3		1
Smith, Dennis, bridge builder, res n Mulberry. -	1	3		1
Smith, Mrs. Sarah, res n Mulberry street. - -		2		
Smith, Charles, laborer, res w Gambier street. -	1	1		
Smith, Frank, druggist, brds at Mrs. Ewalt's, cor Gambier and Gay streets. - - -	1			
Smith, William L., painter, res s Gay street. -	2	2	1	1
SMITHISLER, PHILIP, (of the firm of Milless & Co., Clothiers,) res w High street. -	1	3		2
Smiley, Samuel, carpet weaver, res Mansfield ave	2	2	1	1
Sister John, } Of the Franciscian Order, }				
Sister Therese, } Teachers of the Catholic Pa- } -		3		
Sister Mary, } rochial School, res e High. }				
SINGER, J. W. F., merchant tailor, N. N. Hill's block, s Main, brds Rowley House. -	1	1		
Singer, G. F., tailor, res Mansfield ave. -	2	2	1	1
Singer, G. W., blacksmith, res n Main street. -	1	2		
Singer, Lucy, res n Main street.				
Snoddy, James, carpenter, res n Norton street. -	1	1		
Snow, Alden, painter, res Sandusky street. -	1	3		2
Snook, Miss May, brds C. L. Bennett's, n Gay st.		1		
Snowden, Mrs., [c] } Snowden Minstrels.				
Snowden, Sophia, [c] } Residence				
Snowden, Benjamin, [c] } near Mansfield road				
Snowden, Lewis, [c] }				
Snyder, Mrs. Margaret, res s Norton street. -		1		
Snyder, John J., policeman, res Reeve's block. -	1	1		
Snyder, Mrs. J. J., dress maker, " "				
Snyder, W. B., carriage ironer, res Adams & High	1	1		
Southmayd, Rev. L,, pastor Christian Church, res Coshocton avenue. - - -	1	2		1
Southwick, Mrs. Eliza, res Chester street. -	1	2	1	1
Sperry, J., & Co., dry goods merchants, Pub. Sqr.				
SPERRY, Jared, (of the above firm, residence north Main street. - - -	1	2		
Sperry, Miss Anna, res n Main street.				
SPERRY, WILMOT, (of the firm J. Sperry & Co., dry goods merchants,) res n Main street.	1	1		

16

Every large Business Man in the City of New York has his Life and Property Insured. Call on *J. J. Fultz, Agt.*	Population.		Minors	
	M	F	M	F
Sperry & Browning, dry goods merchants, s Main				
SPERRY, ORLO, (of the above firm,) res corner Main and Burgess streets. - - -	1	3		
Sperry, Nanny, res cor Main and Burgess streets.				
Sperry, William S., clerk, res Main and Burgess.	1			
Spencer, William H., clerk in auditor's office, C. Mt. V. & C. R.R., res e Plimpton street. -	1	3		2
Spearman, John, farmer, res Delaware road.				
Spearman, Thomas, gardener, res e Gambier st. -	3	5	2	4
Spindler, J. C., draughtsman, res Gay & Burgess.	2	4	1	3
Stamp, Mrs. Dr. M. W., res e Gambier street. --		1		
Stamp, M. W., commercial traveler, e Gambier.	1			
Starr, N. B., nursery man, res Gambier road.				
Starr, Miss DeVilla, " " "				
Starr, " Mary,				
STAHL, GEORGE W., dealer in Fancy Notions, &c., e side Pub. Sqr., res High & McKenzie.	2	2	1	1
Stahl, Miss Minnie, " " "				
Stahl, George, " " "				
Starke, Frederick, postal clerk, res Coshocton ave	1			
Stanton, James B., sewing mach. agt., res n Gay.	4	2	3	1
Stanton, R. D., carpenter, " " -	1			
Stilley, Gilman B., farmer, res Delaware road.				
Stilley, Morgan, " " "				
SPRAGUE, S. ANSON, boot and shoemaker, e Gambier, near Main, res e Hamtramck st. -	2	1	1	
SPRAGUE, E. H., machine and job repairer, shop and residence cor Mulberry & Chestnut.	1	1		
Sproule, Joseph, grocer, n Main, res e Gambier st.	1	3		
Sproule, Miss Iva M., " "				
Steam Fire Engine and Hose Cos., e side Gay, between High and Chestnut.				
Stevenson, Henry, laborer, res Coshocton avenue.	3	3	2	2
Stevenson, John G., shipping clerk with C. & G. Cooper & Co., res w Chestnut st. - -	2	2	1	1
Stevens, Mrs. E. E., res cor Sugar and Gay sts. -	1	4	1	1
Stevens, Belle, " " "				
Stevens, Rosa. " " "				
STEVENS, JOHN H., Grain, Flour and Wool Dealer, warehouse foot of Main street, res cor Sugar and Gay streets. - - - -	3	1	2	
Stevens, U. O., book keeper for the above, res cor Sugar and Gay streets. - - - - -	1			
Stephens & Fowler, dentists, Kirk Hall.				
STEPHENS, ROBERT, (of the above firm,) res w High street. - - - - -	3	1	2	
Stephens, Harrison, teacher, res Mansfield ave. -	3	4	2	1
Stephens, Flora, " " "				

Insure Yourselves in the C. M. L. & H. I. Co., of Mt. Vernon, O.	Popu-lation.		Minors	
	M	F	M	F
Stephens, F. A., saddler, res e Chestnut street.	1			
Steele, Mrs. Mary E., res near s Harrison street.	1	2	1	1
Steele, Geo. W., ex-Sheriff, res e Gambier "	1	1		
Steinheuer, G. W., marble cutter, res w Gambier.	2	1	1	
Stewart, John S., clerk, res e High street.	1			
Stallo, Frank, cabinet maker, res Sugar & West.	2	1	1	
Stauffer & Son, Clothiers, cor Main and Pub. Sqr.				
Stauffer, Joseph, (of the above,) res cor Mulberry and Plimpton streets.	1	1		
Stauffer, A. F., (of the above,) res n Mulberry st.	1	2		1
Stone, Mrs. Elizabeth, res n Main street.		1		
Stone, Dan C., postal clerk, res n Main street.	1	4		3
Stokes, A., wagon maker, res Norton & Burgess.	6	3	5	1
Stokes, Isaac S., boiler maker, res " "	1			
Stokes, Geo. S., wagon maker, " " "	1			
Stoeckle, Joseph F., clerk, res e Front street.	1	1		
Stout, Jonathan S., pat. maker, res w Chestnut.	2	2	1	1
STOYLE, HARRY, stone mason, res Harkness road.				
Stinemates, Mollie, help at Rowley House.		1		
Stinemates, Samuel, brick and stone mason, res corner Front and McKenzie streets.	1	2		
Stinemates, John, farmer, res near Columbus road				
Stinemates, John, carpenter, res Boynton street.	5	2	4	1
STRICKLE, ISAAC, with Chase & Cassil, book merchants, s Main, res e High street.	1			
Sturts, Levi, mill-wright, res cor High & West.	2	2	1	
STYRES, JACOB, teamster with C. A. Bope, coal dealer, res cor Gambier & Walnut sts.	1	1		
STYRES, JACOB M., clerk with J. M. Andrews s Main, res e Front.	1	2		1
STURGES, FRED. D., cashier First National Bank, res e Gambier street.	2	4	1	2
Sturges, Millie, res e Gambier street.				
Sturges, Ella R., " e "				
Sturges, H. A., clerk 1st Nat. Bk., res e Gambier.	1			
Sunderland, Richard, butcher, res n Mulberry st.	6	3	5	2
Sutton, Richard, laborer, res e Plimpton street.	4	3	3	2
Sutton, Thomas, Sr., miller, res Sugar & Norton.	2	3	1	1
Sutton, Thomas, Jr., cooper, " " "	1			
Swetland, J. C. & Co., dry goods merchants, cor Main and Gambier streets.				
Swetland, J. C., (of the above,) res Morrow co.				
Swetland, B. L., (of the above,) " w Chestnut st.	1	3		1
Swetland, H. C., clerk with above, res w "	1			
Swetland, Mary, res w Chestnut street.				
Swetland, Catharine, res w Chestnut street.				
Swikert, Philip, barber, brds Central House.	1			

	Popu-lation.		Minors	
	M	F	M	F

T

TAYLOR, Dr. Z. E., resident dentist, s Main, over Russell's drug store, res e Gambier st. -	2	2	1	1
TAYLOR, J. W., druggist, cor Main & Chestnut streets, boards with Mrs. Maj. Sapp, e High.	1			
TAYLOR, HUGH, superintendent Gas Works, res e Front street. - - - - -	3	1	2	
Taylor, William R., laborer, res e Chestnut street	3	2	2	1
TAYLOR, SAMUEL, cooper, residence west Vine, near Norton's mill race. - - -	1	2		1
Taylor, Charles A., cooper, res w Vine street. -	1			
Taylor, Emmanuel, cabinet maker, res s Harrison	5	2	4	1
Taylor, John, laborer, res s Harrison street. -	1			
Taylor, Henry, cooper, " w Gambier " -	1	1		
Taylor, W. G., " " w " " -	4	3	3	2
Taylor, S. L., adjuster for Knox Mu., res n Main.	3	3	2	1
Taylor, George B., res n Main street. - -	1			
Taylor, Edward R., " " "				
Taylor, Fanny, " " "				
Taft, H. C. & Co., dealers in books & stationery, Woodward Hall, cor Main and Vine streets				
TAFT, H. C., (of the above firm,) res e Gambier, near Center run. - - - -	2	2	1	
Taft, J. G., (of the above firm,) res e Gambier st.	1			
Taft, H. C. & Co.'s Circulating Library, Woodward Hall, cor Main and Vine streets.				
Tathwell, W. A., baker, shop and res w Vine st.	1	4		3
Tathwell, Mrs. Mary Ann, res e Plimpton street.		1		
Tathwell, Mrs. Ellen, " e "		1		
Tathwell, William, gardener, res n Mulberry st.	1	1		
Tate, Jackson, [c] laborer, res e Vine street. -	3	3	2	2
Taugher, Michael, " " w Vine " -	3	3	2	2
Taugher, Patrick, " " e Hamtramck st. -	4	3	3	3
Taugher, Thomas, " " e Plimpton street.	1	1		
Taugher, Jeremiah, " " e " " -	2	1	1	
Tarr, A. B., res cor Mulberry and Hamtramck. -	2	1	1	
Tarr, H. P., dealer in boots and shoes, in Miller's block, e side s Main, res w Chestnut street.	2	1	1	
Teeters, Mrs. Caroline, res n Mulberry street. -	1	3	1	2
Teeters, John S., laborer, res n " "	1			
Terry, Freeborn, watchman R. R. crossings, res e Gambier street. - - - - -	1	1		
Terry, Warner, res cor Chestnut & Coshocton sts.	2	2	1	
Terry, Joanna, " " "				
Terry, Caroline, " " "				
Terry, E. W., painter, res Chestnut & Coshocton.	1			

	Popu-lation.		Minors	
The life of Horace Greeley was insured for one hundred thousand dollars. Call on J. J. Fultz, Agt.	M	F	M	F
Terry, B. L., mail agt., brds with Dr. Pumphrey.				
Thayer, Alfred, machinist, res n Norton street. -	3	2	2	
Tibbs, John, [c] barber, res High & Mechanic sts.	1			
Tiffany, J. W. H., laborer, res Sandusky street. -	1	1		
Tighe, James, moulder, res w Sugar street. -	8	3	7	2
Tivna, Hugh, laborer, res w Vine street. - -	1	1		
Tinder, Mrs. Agnes, res e Sugar street. - -		1		
Tims, William, car repairer, res e Water street. -	2	1	1	
Tilton, Rev. A. H., res e Plimpton street. -	1	1		
TILTON, J. A., Gen. Frt. & Ticket Agent, C. Mt. V. & C. R.R., res n Mulberry street. -	4	1	3	
Tilton & Armstrong, Grocers and Provision Merchants, old Masonic Hall, s Main street.				
Tilton, G. H., (of the above,) res Main & Plimpton	2	4	1	2
Thrap, Rev. J. A., pastor Methodist Church, res Parsonage, n Mulberry street. - - -	1			
THOMPSON, JOHN D., Treasurer C. Mt. V. & C. R.R., res cor Sugar & Mulberry streets. -	1	1		
Thompson, Rev. Wm., Pastor Protestant Episcopal Church, res e Chestnut street. -	1	1		
THOMPSON, S. C., physician, s Main, over Dr. Ward's drug store, res e Water st. - -	2	2	1	1
Thompson, Robert, dealer in agricultural implements, res e Gambier street. - - -	1	3		1
Thompson, Miss Carrie, res e Gambier street.		1		
Thompson, " Martha, brds at J. Ponting's, e Gambier street. - - - -		1		
Thompson, Mrs. Dr. Matthew, res n Main street.		4		2
Thompson, Miss Mame, " "				
Thompson, " Annie, " "				
Thompson, Thomas J., salesman with Millers & Co., Clothiers, Kirk Hall, res w Chestnut. -	1			
Thompson, Mrs. Agnes, " " -		2		
Thompson, Miss Aggie, " "				
THOMPSON, WM. M., saddle and harness maker, north side Pub. Sqr., res s Mulberry. -	3		2	
Thomson, William A., printer, res e Vine street.	1	1		
Thomas, David, farmer, res e Vine street. -	1			
Thomas, Mrs. Rebecca, " s Norton street. -	1	2	1	1
Thomas, Chris., blacksmith, res s Mulberry st. -	1			
Thomas, Levi, baggage master, C. Mt. V. & C. R. R. depot, res e Front street. - - -	1			
Thomas, Truman, cabinet maker, res w Gambier.	3	1	2	
Thomas, Henry, [c] laborer, res s Mulberry st. -	1			
Thomas, Mrs. Mary, [c] " " -	2	4	2	2
TOMLINSON, E. J., saddle and harness maker, n side Public Square, res e Chestnut st. -	1	3		2
Tompkins, J. M., residence e Gambier street. -	1	1		

Every Young Business Man should have his Life and Property insured. J. J. Fultz. Agt.	Popu-lation.		Minors	
	M	F	M	F
Torrey, O. D., traveling salesman, res s Mulberry	3	2	2	1
Third Ward School House, n side e Chestnut btw Gay and McKenzie streets.				
Travis, David L., res Wooster avenue. - - -	1	2		
Tress, James, machinist, res Mansfield avenue. -	1			
Tress, Mrs. Mary, " " " -		2		
Tress, Miss Mary, " " "				
TRICK, THOMAS, boot maker, Miller's block, s Main, res e Lamartin street. - - -	3	4	2	2
Trick, Miss Alice, res e Lamartin street.				
Trick, " Selina, " " " "				
Trimble, Thomas H., farmer, res Mansfield ave.	1	1		
Trimble, John, " " "	1	4		
Trimble, Emma, teacher, " " "				
Trimble, Elizabeth, " " "				
Trimble, Anna, " " "				
Trimble, Asa M., book keeper, " "	1			
Trimble, John N., Engr., C. & T. R.R. " "	1			
Trimble, Wm. E., wagon maker, " "	1			
TROTT, SAMUEL A., baker, shop and residence Mansfield avenue. - - -	1	2		1
Trott, Miss Emma, res Mansfield avenue.				
Trott, William, machinist, res Columbus road.				
True, John, farmer, res Mulberry and Plimpton.	1	2		1
True, Mrs. John J., res e Front street. - - -		1		
Tulloss, Mrs. Felicia, teacher, res Wooster ave. -	1	1	1	
TULLOSS, R. S., Justice Peace, res Morgan tp. Member Constitutional Convention, 1873.				
Turner, Robert, farmer, res Delaware road.				
TURNER, WILLIAM, Secretary Knox Mutual Insurance Company, res n Main street. - -	1	2		
Turner, Julia, " n " "				
Turner, George J., mail agent, C. Mt. V. & C. R. R., res n Gay street. - - - -	2	2	1	
Tousley, Mrs. Ellen, res s Mulberry street. -		1		
Tousley, John W., moulder, res s Mulberry st. -	1			
Trumbull, Mrs. Emeline, res w Chestnut street. -		1		
Trumbull, Alex., carriage maker, res w High st.	1	2		1
Tuch, Moses, clerk with Leopold, res Vine & Gay	1		1	
Tudor, Henry, grocer Sandusky st., res Cox's Hill				
Tudor, John, res cor Gay and Sugar streets. -	1	4		1
Tudor, Ida, " " " "				
Tudor, Clara, " " " "				
TUDOR, BENJAMIN F., meat market, n Main near Chestnut, boards at Bergin House. -	1	1		
Tuller, W., dry goods merchant, Woodbridge's old stand, s Main, brds at Mrs. Buckland's.	1			

	Popu-lation.		Minors	
	M	F	M	F

U

Union (or High) School Building, corner Mulberry and Hamtramck streets.

Upfold, Alfred, boiler maker, res Railroad street.	2	2	1	1
UPDEGRAFF, PERCIVAL A., res Granville road.				
Updegraff, Miss Mary, res w Chestnut street.	-	1		
Urquhart, Moses, soap manufacturer, res e Vine.	2	4	1	2
Underwood, Israel, ex-Sheriff, res e Chestnut st.	1	2		
Underwood, Miss Jennie, " "				

V

VANCE, WALTER L., Constable, residence e Gambier street. -	2	2	1	1
Vance, Al., residence e Gambier street. -	1			
Vance, Miss Sadie, " " -		1		
Vance, " Ella, " " -		1		
Vance, Agnew, ear trimmer, res e Front street. -	2	4	1	3
Vance, Scott, horse trainer, res Vine & Mulberry.	1			
Vance, Miss Maria, " " "		1		
VAN AKIN, C. W., dealer in boots, shoes, hats, caps, furs, &c., Kirk Hall, res n Main street.	2	3	1	1
Veatch, Miss E. A., brds at Dr. Pickard's, w High		1		
Veatch, E., drayman, res s Mechanic street.	1	3		1
Ventling, Cyrus, farmer, res near Columbus road				
Ventling, Jonathan, farmer, res Sparta road.				
Vernon, Mrs. Rachael, res cor Main & Gambier.	1	1	1	
VINCENT, EDWARD, druggist with Dr. J. W. Taylor s Main, res Cemetery avenue. -	2	1	1	
Vohl, Fred W., butcher, res Clinton township.				
Vohl, Miss Sadie, brds with Peter Hoke, e High.		1		1
Vohl, " Eva, " " " "		1		1
VORE, GEORGE M., Boot Maker, Banning Hall, brds with Mrs. Booze, s Mulberry street	1			

W

Waddell, John, res w High street. -	1	1		
Wade, Major, [c] laborer, res cor High & Norton.	1	1		
Walker, Uriah, farmer, res Mansfield road.				
Walker, Samuel H., [c] laborer, res w Vine st. -	3	1	2	
Walter, G. W., carpenter, res s Catharine street.	6	3	5	2
Walters, W. J., lumberman, res w Vine street. -	1	2		1

17

G. W. MORGAN,
ATTORNEY-AT-LAW,
MOUNT VERNON, OHIO.

☞ Particular attention paid to Collections in all parts of the United States.

Office—In Kirk Opera House.

WILLIAM DUNBAR.   JOHN J. LENNON.

DUNBAR & LENNON,
Attorneys-At-Law
AND
NOTARIES PUBLIC,
Mt. Vernon, Ohio.

OFFICE—Three Doors north of First National Bank, over Hills' Queensware Store, south Main street.

☞ Will attend promptly to all legal business, including Pensions and Patents, intrusted to them in Knox and adjoining Counties.

C. E. CRITCHFIELD,
Attorney-At-Law,
MT. VERNON, OHIO.

☞ Collections promptly attended to. Special attention paid to all matters in connection with settlement of estates.

OFFICE—In the Old Masonic Hall, south Main street, over ARMSTRONG & TILTON'S Store.

C. D. HYLER,
JUSTICE OF THE PEACE & NOTARY PUBLIC,
FREDERICKTOWN, OHIO.

Prompt attention paid to Collections.

Every Farmer, Mechanic, and Laborer, should have his Life and Property insured. J. J. Fultz represents Standard Companies.

	Population.		Minors	
	M	F	M	F
Walsh, Thomas, miller, res n Norton street. -	1	1		
WALLACE, JAMES R., plasterer, residence n Gay street. - - - - - - -	2	1	1	
Wallace, Albert D., plasterer, brds Central House	1			
Wagoner, Mrs. Mary E., dress maker, over Stauffer's clothing store, n side Public Square. -		1		
Wagoner, Miss Ella, dress maker, with above. -		1		
WARD, Dr. TRUMAN, Druggist, w side south Main, res e High street. - - - -	1	2		
Ward, Miss Victoria, res e High street.				
Ward, Byron, brick mason, res e High street. -	3	1	2	
Ward, F. F. & Co., Jewelers, s e cor Main & Vine				
Ward, L. B., (of the above firm,) res e Gambier.	3	2	2	
Ward, F. F., (of the above firm,) " -	1			
Ward, C. C., farmer, res Green Valley road.				
Ward, H. P., carriage maker, brds Rowley House	1			
Ward, Alonzo, machinist, res n West street. -	2	4	1	3
Warner, Mrs. Anne, res Sandusky street. - -		2		1
Warren, J. B., blacksmith, shop & res n Mechanic	1	2		1
Washington, Austin, [c] laborer, res w Vine. -	1			
Washington, John, [c] " " " -	1			
Washington, Elias, [c] " " w Chestnut.	2	2	1	1
Watson & Wood, attorneys, Kremlin Block.				
WATSON, JOSEPH, (of the above firm,) res e High street. - - - - - -	5	2	4	
Watson, William B., carpenter, res e High. -	1			
Watson, J. S., editor Sunbury Spectator.				
Watson, J. H., associate editor "				
Watson, S. W., Fashionable Millinery, s Main, near Woodbridge's old stand, res n Gay.	1	3		
Watkins, Mrs. Eliza, res Cemetery avenue. -	4	1	4	
Watkins, Miss Abby, fine art store, w Gambier		1		
Watkins, A. H., " " " " res Cemetery avenue.	1			
Watkins, Frank, commercial traveler, residence n Mulberry. - - - - - - -	1	2		1
Watkins, Miss Eliza, res Mansfield road.				
Wayne, Mrs. Esther, brds with W. McClelland, e High. -		2		1
WEAVER, JONATHAN, Grocer, 102 s Main, res same. - - - - - -	1	2		
Weaver, Charles F., clerk, res 102 s Main. -	1			
Weaver, Frank, book keeper, res 102 s Main. -	1	2		1
Weaver, Mrs. Adam, res e High. - - -		3		1
WEAVER, SAMUEL P., tailor, with J. W. F. Singer, s Main, res n West street. - -	2	4	1	
WEAVER, CHRISTIAN, boot & shoemaker, s Main, below Gambier, res n Gay. - -	2	3	1	2
Weaver, Lavina, res n Gay.				

Insure Yourselves in the C. M. L. & H. I. Co., of Mt. Vernon, O.

	Population.		Minors	
	M	F	M	F
Weaver, Wm. B., shoemaker, res s Main.	1	1		
Weaver, Monroe, huckster, res n Mulberry.	1			
WEEKS, CARLOS H., Manager Telegraph Office, Kirk Hall, res e Vine.	1	1		
Weeks, Homer A., telegraph operator, C. Mt. V. & C. R.R. depot, res e Vine.	1			
Weeks, Thomas, dentist, brds with Mrs Buckland	1			
Weber, Mrs. Charles, res n Gay.	4	2	1	
WEBER, FRED., baker, bakery and residence cor Vine and Adams streets.	3	3	2	2
Weber, Lavina Elizabeth, res cor Vine & Adams.				
Weber, Mary Matilda, " " " "				
WEIGHT, J. B., attorney, Banning Hall, res n Main.	1			
Weirick, Henry S., clerk, res High & Norton.	1	1		
Weirick, Clifford, clerk C. Mt. V. & C. R.R., res cor High and Norton.	1		1	
Weirick, James, tanner, res Vine and Harrison.	2	1	1	
WEILL, SAMUEL, dealer in Furs & Peltries, res s Main.	1	1		
Welshymer, Otho, teamster, res Sandusky street.	1	3		1
Welshymer, Charles, " " "	1			
Welshymer, Jefferson, machinist, res e Curtis.	1	2		1
Welsh, John, farmer, res new Delaware road.				
Welsh, Reason, " " Columbus & Sparta road				
Welsh, Marion, florist, seed & fruit grower,)				
Welsh, Marion, Ice Cream Parlors,	1	2		1
res cor Main street & Wooster avenue)				
Welsh, Steven, res e Plimpton.	1			
Welsh, James, machinist, res Sandusky.	1			
Welsh, Mrs. Peter, restaurant & boarding house, s side e Gambier, between Main and Gay.	3	2	3	
Welker, C., clerk with F. W. Miller, s Main, res n Mulberry.	1	2	1	
Wells, Mrs. Mary A., res w Vine.	1	1	1	
Wells, Mrs. Emma B. res e Chestnut.		2		
Wells, Miss Bessie, teacher, res e Chestnut.		1		
Westlick, James, res n Norton.	1	2		1
WEST, RICHARD F., cutter with Milless & Co., Clothiers, res Gambier & McArthur.	3	2	2	
Wiant, Rev. A. J., Baptist clergyman, res e Vine	4	2	3	1
Wiant, Andrew, farmer, res e Gambier.	1			
Wilkins, Frank, res cor Water and East.	1	4		
Wilkins, Miss Allie, " " " "				
Wilkins, John, painter, " " "	1			
Wilkerson, Henry E., clerk Oil Mill, res w Vine.	4	1	3	
Wilcox, Geo. L., tailor, Woodward Hall, res Sandusky street.	3	3	2	2

	Popu-lation.		Miners	
Every Young Business Man should have his Life and Property insured. J. J. Fultz, Agt.	M	F	M	F
Willis, W. C., (of McCormick, Willis & Banning, furniture dealers,) res w Chestnut. -	1	2		1
Willis, Miss Elizabeth, " "				
Willis, " Fannie, " "				
Wilson, John, farmer, res Green Valley road.				
Wilson, Henry C., " " " "				
Wilson, Philip, tanner & currier, res w Chestnut.	1	2		1
Wilson, Robert G., farmer, " "	1			
Wilson, Edward J., medical student, res " -	1			
Wilson, Allen, plasterer, res s Catharine. -	1	2		1
Wilson, J. R., farmer, res Morris township.				
Wilson, John, gardener, res e Gambier. -	1	1		
Wilson, Thomas, engineer C. Mt. V. & C. R. R., res s McArthur. - - - -	1	3		2
Wilson, Rufus, stone mason, res Madison street.	1			
Wilson, Perry, [c] laborer, res Railroad street. -	2	2	1	1
Williams, William, laborer, res w Hamtramck. -	1	1		
Williams, Nahum, Sr., dairy man, res Sandusky.	1	1		
Williams, Mrs. Nahum, Jr., res Sandusky. -		2		1
Williams, Cornelius, brakeman B. & O., Sandusky	1			
Williams, Edward D., painter, res e Sugar. -	1	2		1
Williams, Albert, wagon maker, res e Front. -	4	1	3	
Williams, Jas., [c] barber, res Front & Mulberry.	3	2	2	1
WING, MELVIN, farmer, Granville road, res corner High and Gay streets. - - -	1	3		
Wing, Miss Maria J., res cor High and Gay.				
Wing, A. J., " " " " -	1			
Wing, William R., farmer, res Granville road.				
Wing, Mrs. A. J., res w Vine. - - -	1	1	1	
Winne, George, res e Chestnut. - - -	1	2		
Winne, Miss Kitty, res e Chestnut.				
Winne, Frank, clerk, with Baldwin, the hatter, res e Chestnut. - - - - -	1			
Winston, R. L., farmer, res Newark road.				
Wintermute, H. O., clerk, res w Chestnut. -	4	3	3	2
WHITE, GEORGE B., Post-Master, res corner High and McKenzie streets. - - -	2	4	1	1
White, Miss Clara, teacher, ⎫				
White, " Hattie, postal clerk, ⎪ Residence				
White, " Ella, ⎬ as				
White, " Maria B., ⎪ above.				
White, Chandler, student, ⎭				
WHITE, JOHN W., Printer and Directory Compiler, res e Chestnut, near McKenzie. -	2	3	1	1
White, Miss Caroline, teacher, ⎫				
White, " Jessie B., ⎬ Res as above.				
White, Arthur Lincoln, student, ⎭				

Every large Business Man in the City of New York has his Life and Property Insured. Call on *J. J. Fultz, Agt.*	Population		Minors	
	M	F	M	F
White, Matthew, stone cutter, res corner Vine & Catharine. - - - - - - -	1	2		1
White, Charles, [c] laborer, res Oak street. - -	2	2	1	1
White, Frank, conductor C. Mt. V. & C. R. R., residence e Front. - - - - -	3	1	2	
White, Albert, laborer, res e Curtis. - -	1	1		
WHITESIDES, NEVILLE P., of John Cooper Manufacturing Co., res Thistle Ridge. -	2	1	1	
Whitehead, Henry, Janitor High School building, res w Pleasant. - - - -	1	3		2
WHITTINGTON, N., Family Grocer, Jones' block, w High, res n West street. -	1	2		1
Whittington, Charles, with above, res n West st.	1	2		1
Whittington, Anthony, machinist, " n Norton.	1	2		1
Whittington, Wm. H., " " cor High & Mechanic. - - - - - -	1	2		1
Whitney, A. A., clerk with Swetland & Co., cor Main and Gambier, res e Gambier. - -	1	1		
Whitney, Mrs. Ann, dress maker, res e Vine. -		2		
Wirt, Mrs. Mary, res cor Main and Pleasant. -		2		
Wirt, John S., cabinet maker, res Main & Pleasant	1	1		
Wirt, J. G., Ice Packer, res Walnut and Vine. -	1	1		
Wheeler, Mrs. Annie, res w Vine. - - -		3		1
Woning, A., tailor, res e Gambier. - - -	3	5	2	4
Wonn, Joseph, machinist, res Sandusky. - -	3	4	2	3
Woodward Opera House, cor Main and Vine sts.				
Woodward, E. G., proprietor of Woodward Opera House, res e Gambier. - - -	2	3	1	1
Woodward, Miss Charlotte, res e Gambier.				
Woodward, Rev. J. M., Methodist Clergyman, res e Lamartin street. - - - -	1	2		
Woodward, G. H., teacher res e Lamartin. -	3	1	2	
Woodhall, Thomas, wrks Gas House, res e High.	1	1		
WOOD, DAVID W., attorney, of the firm of Watson & Wood, res Mansfield avenue. -	1	1		
Wood, Isaac, brick maker, res e Burgess. - -	1	2		
Wood, Thomas, " " " - -	1	1		
Wood, James H., " " " - -	1			
Wood, Jefferson, teamster, " e Plimpton. - -	2	2	1	1
Worl, Fred., tailor, res Rogers street. - -	1	1		
WORLEY, JAMES, proprietor Worley House, cor High and Norton streets. - - -	1	1		
WOLFFE, A., Clothier, Banning block, corner Main and Vine, res e Gambier. - - -	2	2	1	1
Wolffe, Charles, clerk, ⎫		1		
Wolffe, Simon, " ⎬ Residence as above.		1		
Wolffe, Morris, " ⎪		1		
Wolffe, Miss Thressa, ⎭		1		

	Popu-lation.		Minors	
	M	F	M	F
Insure Yourselves and Property with **J. J. FULTZ, Agent.**				
Wolf, Mrs. Henrietta, res s Mulberry. - -		3		
Wolf, Caarles, tinner, " " - - -	1			
Wolf, Frank, machinist, res e Chestnut. - -	1	3		2
Wolf, William, tinner, res e Hamtramck. - -	3	1	2	
Work, J. D., farmer, res Fredericktown road.				
Wright, Chancey, wrks Oil Mill, res w Gambier.	2	4	1	3
Wright, John, [c] laborer, res High & Mechanic.	1			
Wright, George, blacksmith, res s Mulberry. -	2	1	1	
Wright, G. W., carpenter, res Front & McKenzie	1	1		
Wright, Miss Martha J., " " "		1		
WRIGHT, E. M., Printer and Constable, res e Front street. - - - - -	1	2		1
Wyker, J. D. S., clerk with J. Sperry & Co., res n Mulberry. - - - - -	1			
Wythe, William, boot maker, res w Front. - -	4	1	3	
Wythe, George, machinist, res w Hamtramck. -	3	3	2	2

Y

Yardley, R. B , painter, boards at Central House.	1			
Yeager, Joseph, cabinet maker, boards at Mrs. Booze's, s Mulberry. - - - -	1			
Young, H. M., dealer in leather, wool, &c., west side Public Square, res e Gambier. - -	1	4		3
Young, Miss May, " "				
YOUNG, WILLIAM M., Jeweler, w side of Main, res e Gambier. - - - -	2	3	1	1
Young, Miss Minne, res e Gambier.				
Young, Silas, farmer, res Coshocton road.				
Young & Bartlett, livery and feed stable, w Vine				
Young, Andrew, (of the above,) res corner Vine and Mechanic streets. - - -	2	2	1	1
Young, Snowden, moulder, res Sandusky street.	1	4		3
Young, Hezekiah, farmer, res Chesterville road.				
Younker, John, brewer, res McKenzie & Water.	2	1	1	
Younker, Jacob, " " Rogers street. - -	1	2		1

Z

ZIMMERMAN, F. J., Grocer, w side s Main, residence e Front. - - - - -	1	1		
Zimmerman, Miss Rose E., res e Front.		1		

THREE SCORE AND TEN!

(— o —)

SHORT BIOGRAPHICAL SKETCHES.

. — .

[THE following brief personal sketches of a few of our aged and venerable citizens were collected during the summer just past, with a view of bringing before our readers the experience and trials of our pioneer settlers.   The limited capacity of our little work will only permit of brief mention.   The sketches are given in the order in which they were obtained.]

I—II.
JOHN AND SARAH CROWL.

Mr. JOHN CROWL, of the Fifth Ward, was born in the then small village of Martinsburgh, Virginia, on the 6th day of April, 1789.   He came to Mount Vernon, Ohio, on the 26th day of November, 1826.   Mr. Crowl has been twice married.   He married his present wife, May 6, 1844.

Mrs. SARAH CROWL, (wife of Mr. John Crowl,) was born in the village of —————, New Jersey, on the 16th day of December, 1793.   She removed to Mount Vernon, Ohio, in the year 1838, and was married to Mr. John Crowl, on the date above mentioned.

18

III.

WILLIAM BURRISS.

Mr. WILLIAM BURRISS, of the Fifth Ward, was born in Lancashire, England, August 6, 1804. Mr. Burriss landed at the New York City Docks on the 20th day of May, 1846. The voyage across the Ocean occupied five weeks. Mr. Burriss started on foot for the Great West, and reached Mount Vernon, Ohio, June 6, 1846. In his youth he learned the trade of blacksmith.

IV.

SAMUEL TAYLOR.

Mr. SAMUEL TAYLOR, of the Second Ward, was born in the town of Troy, State of New York, on the 14th day of April, 1800. Mr. Taylor removed to Mount Vernon, Ohio, on the 7th day of June, 1839, and has been a resident of the place ever since. During a residence of thirty-seven years, he has lived in only four houses—thirty-five of the thirty-seven years, he has spent in his present residence. By profession Mr. Taylor is a cooper.

V.

NANCY ROBINSON.

Mrs. NANCY ROBINSON, (the mother of Mrs. Jacob Earnest,) of the Fourth Ward, was born December 25, 1792, near Frostburg, Maryland. In Ohio, she first located at Danville, Knox county, and came to Mount Vernon, October 16, 1866.

VI.

SAMUEL DUNCAN.

Mr. SAMUEL DUNCAN, of the Second Ward, was born in Doylestown, Pennsylvania, on the —— day of April, 1801. Mr. Duncan came to Ohio when 20 years of age. The exact date of his arrival in Mount Vernon is unknown, but he claims to have resided here thirty-two years. Accurate dates in Mr. Duncan's career could not be obtained, as no record of events was kept by his family.

VII.

DANIEL McGRADY.

Mr. DANIEL McGRADY, of the Fourth Ward, was born November ——, 1792, in Londonderry, Ireland. He came to New York city in the year 1816, and to Mount Vernon, O., September 15, 1838. Mr. McGrady served three years as a private in the British Army prior to his emigration to America.

VIII—IX.
JACOB AND NANCY BOOZE.

Mr. JACOB BOOZE, of the Second Ward, was born August 10, 1796, in the county of Washington, Penn. He first came to Mount Vernon, June 7, 1831. Mr. Booze has been married three times, and is the father of thirteen children, eleven of whom are still living—eight in Ohio, (three in Knox county,) one in Indiana, and two in Missouri. He married Miss Nancy Byers, (his third wife,) December 7, 1850.

Mrs. NANCY BOOZE, (wife of Jacob Booze,) was born January 29, 1807, in Harrison county, Ohio, within a few miles of Cadiz, the county seat. She came to Knox county in April, 1822; married Mr. Booze December 7, 1850, and took up her residence in Mount Vernon in April, 1874.

X.
GEORGE C. LYBRAND.

Mr. GEORGE C. LYBRAND, of the First Ward, was born June 16, 1792, in the city of Philadelphia, Pa. He came to Mount Vernon in April, 1823. In the earlier days of our city, Mr. Lybrand took a prominent part, and was, at one time, an active and energetic merchant. His means were freely used, not so much for his own immediate aggrandisement, as for the growth and prosperity of the place of his adoption. The "Lybrand House," (now known as the "Rowley House,") was, at the time of its erection, considered one of the most extensive public buildings in Central Ohio; this house, and the large brick tenement block located on east Front street, are standing monuments of his public spirit and enterprise.

XI—XII.
JOHN AND MARY MILLER.

Mr. JOHN MILLER, of the Fourth Ward, was born June 9, 1790, in Fredericktown, Maryland. He married Miss Mary Deems, of Cumberland, Md., July —, 1822. He came to Mount Vernon, August 10, 1835.

Mrs. MARY MILLER, (nee Deems,) was born July 28, 1802, in Cumberland, Md. She married Mr. Miller, at the time stated above, and came to Mount Vernon with her husband in 1835.

XIII.
ALBERT MITCHELL.

Mr. ALBERT MITCHELL, of the First Ward, was born on the 31st day of October, 1805, in the village of Blandford, Mass. On seeking a home in the Great West, his father came to Ohio, and located in Granville, Licking county, November 1st, 1806, when Albert was a little over one year of age. Albert came to Knox county in April, 1824, and in May, 1825, he located in this place, and Mount Vernon has been his home ever since.

XIV.

WILLIAM FORDNEY.

Mr. WILLIAM FORDNEY, of the Fifth Ward, although not strictly coming under the head of "Three Score and Ten," as to age, yet his long residence in Mount Vernon justly entitles him to a place with those more venerable in age. For forty-two years this city has been his abiding place, forty-one of those forty-two years have been spent in his present home, on upper Mulberry street. For the first years of his residence here, it was not unusual for him to stand in the back door of his house of a morning and shoot enough rabbits for breakfast and dinner, for between Mulberry street and the Sandusky road was a dense forest of trees and hazel bushes, the latter so closely packed as to prevent the passage of any thing larger than the smaller wild animals then so numerous. If appetite demanded a change of flesh for food, Mr. Fordney had only to change position and go east, for between Mulberry and Main street, was another forest, abounding with squirrels, many of whom fell victims to his gun. Mount Vernon in 1834, although at that date quite a thriving town, and Mount Vernon in 1876, so far as permanent improvements are concerned, none but the earlier settlers have a correct idea of the vast contrast between the two periods named.

Mr. Fordney was born in the town of Lancaster, Pennsylvania, on the 21st day of January, 1812. In 1833 he married Miss Ann Barber Nagle, also of Lancaster, Penn. On the 28th day of November, 1834, he and his wife cast their lot with the people of this city. Mrs. Fordney died in this city on the 5th day of June, 1859. To them were born eight children, five of whom are still living.

XV.

RUSSELL T. CRANDALL.

Mr. RUSSELL T. CRANDALL, of the Fifth Ward, was born in the town of Burlington, Unadilla county, New York, on the 5th of January, 1802. Mr. Crandall came to Knox county, Ohio, in the year 1829. In the spring of 1876, Mr. C. was elected assessor for the Fifth Ward.

XVI.

NANCY HALL.

Mrs. NANCY HALL, of the Second Ward, was born January 1, 1798, in Shenendoah county, Virginia, near Aspey Ferry. She came to Mount Vernon in 1872.

XVII.

MARY CARTER.

Mrs. MARY CARTER, of the Fifth Ward, was born in Georgetown, (now a part of the District of Columbia,) June 22, 1805. Mrs. Carter came to Knox county, Ohio, in 1840.

XVIII.
JANE HENEGAN.

Mrs. JANE HENEGAN, *nee* Miss Jane Shaw, of the Third Ward, was born on the 10th day of March, 1804, in Sixside, near Carron Hill, Parish of Old Monkland, Lanarkshire, Scotland. On the —— day of ——————, 18—, she married Mr. William Henegan, of the Parish of Killmackshalgan, county of Sligo, Ireland. Mr. H. was born on the 4th day of February, 1803, and died at Keokuk, Iowa, on the 17th day of August, 1870. Mr. and Mrs. H., with their family, came to Mount Vernon in 1853.

The subject of this brief sketch, with her husband and family, left Glasgow, Scotland, September 16, 1849—Liverpool, England, September 18, and arrived at New Orleans, U. S. A., on the 20th day of December following, thus the voyage, between the port of departure, and the port of dis-embarkation, appears to have been thirteen weeks and four days in duration. To vary the interest, and to add to the perils of those "who go down to the sea in ships," we find that the vessel, upon whose deck the lives and fortunes of our hardy emigrants were placed, was castaway in a storm, and thrown upon the shores of an island now called Concon, situated near the barren coast of Yucatan, South America. The passengers and crew were detained twenty-eight days upon that desert island.

During their forced residence upon the island, the passengers and crew, imitating the people of the country in which most of them were seeking a new home, organized a government and made laws for their own protection, and unanimously elected Mr. William Henegan the first Governor of the State of Concon, South America. The necessity of this organization was soon apparent.

The island of Concon, for its favorable and safe harbors, was one of the favorite rendezvous of the piratical vessels making those waters their cruising grounds. One of those sea rovers passing the island, the captain seeing the wrecked ship of our emigrants, determined to take possession, rob it of all the rigging and stores left upon it, (the passengers and crew, while waiting for rescue, living in tents upon the shore.)

To allay suspicion, the pirates also landed, and pitched their tents a short distance from those of our shipwrecked friends, as though they wished to rest awhile from their bloody and murderous career. One of the crew of the wrecked ship, wandering over the island one day, being aweary from his long and difficult tramp, threw himself down behind some rocks, and fell asleep. How long he had remained in that unconscious state he knew not. He was finally awakened, by hearing voices in conversation, apparently, immediately above him. Listening for awhile, he gathered enough of their conversation, to convince him that the voices belonged to some of the crew of the piratical vessel, and that the rascals were detailing to themselves their plans for attacking the unfortunate voyagers and sacking the wrecked vessel. After the departure of the loquacious pirates, the sailor made his way to his own camp, and detailed the plot of the pirates to Governor Henegan.

After a consultation with his Council, the Governor formed his plans of retaliation, which were to capture the pirate vessel, and put to sea with his little colony. This was "carrying the war into Africa," with a vengeance, yet, under the circumstances, was perfectly justifiable.

The Governor's plans were well laid, and would have been successfully carried out, had not one of the passengers betrayed the Governor's plans to the pirate chief. The pirates immediately struck their tents, and began their retreat to their boats, and thence to their vessel. In the melee that ensued, the pirate captain was wounded so severely, as to compel his crew to take him upon their shoulders. In this condition, with their helpless captain, the pirates reached their boats and made for their vessel. When upon her deck, they hoisted their sails, and put out to sea, leaving our shipwrecked friends in possession of their diminutive Republic, and like Alexander Selkirk, they could say—

> " We are monarchs of all we survey,
> Our rights there are none to dispute."

Mrs. Henegan is now residing with her son John, on east High Street, the only survivor of nine children.

Of Mr. William Henegan, permit me to say a few words. Mr. H. commenced Rail Roading at the age of 18, and so continued up to the time of his death, in 1870. He was Superintendent of Construction over many Railroads, both in Scotland and in England, and acted in that capacity for the first Railroad ever built. In the construction of the Cleveland, Mt. Vernon and Columbus R. R., Mr. H. took an active part, and his labors at that time were highly appreciated. The road was then known as the Springfield, Mt. Vernon & Pittsburgh R. R. Hard times came, and the work on the road was suspended. Nearly three and twenty years passed ere the work on the road, under the new organization, was resumed. Under the auspices of the new Company, his son John completed laying the track, between Sunbury and Kinderhook, the job his father had commenced twenty-three years previous.

XIX.

WILLIAM BROADHURST.

Mr. WILLIAM BROADHURST, of the Fourth Ward, was born May 10, 1798, in the village of Bolton, Lancashire county, England. He emigrated to America in 1816, leaving the English docks on the 21st day of March, and arriving in Philadelphia on the 11th day of May, making the voyage seven weeks and two days. Mr. B. has been twice married, his first wife being Miss Isabella McCreary, of Steubenville, Ohio, to whom he was married on the 12th day of April, 1823. His second and present wife was Mrs. Louisa C. Bates, of St. Louis, Missouri, to whom he was married on the 10th day of December, 1865.

XX.

THOMAS EVANS.

Mr. Thomas Evans, of the Fourth Ward, was born on the 24th day of July, 1797, in Berks county, Pennsylvania. He removed to Northumberland county, same State, in 1812. From Northumberland county, he came to Ohio, in 1841, and settled in Mount Vernon, and has resided in the city or immediate vicinity ever since.

Mr. Evans has been married four times, and has had born unto him twelve children—by his first wife two—by his second wife nine—and by his third wife one. Five of his children are still living, and all are residents of Ohio. Three reside in the town of Delaware, one in Morrow county, and one in Knox county. Thomas Evans, Jr., of Delaware, is proprietor of "The Signal," an ardent advocate for a political Prohibition party, and was, at the late Presidential election, the Prohibition elector for this, the 9th, Ohio district.

The fourth wife of Mr. Evans, was Mrs. Naomi Young, widow of Lewis Young, of this city. This last marriage was celebrated in September, 1855.

XXI.

JOSEPH JACOBS.

Mr. Joseph Jacobs, of the Fourth Ward, was born September 25, 1802, in Philadelphia, Pa. Mr. Jacobs removed to Newark, Ohio, in 1833—from thence to Granville, Ohio, 1834,—and from thence to Mount Vernon in 1835. Mr. Jacobs has been married twice. His first wife was Miss Elizabeth Pholeman, of Philadelphia, and his second was Miss Eliza James, of Ohio.

XXII.

GEORGE ADAMS.

Mr. George Adams, of the First Ward, is by profession a wagon maker, and continued to work at it until about a year since. He was born on the 25th March, 1798, in the village of Rushangles, county of Suffolk, England. On the 26th day of March, 1820, he married Miss Elizabeth Harnwell, of Bressingham, county of Norfolk, England. There were born unto Mr. Adams and his wife Elizabeth, thirteen children, five of whom died between the ages of one and three years. Mr. Adams and his family emigrated to America in the year 1852. They left England on the 27th of May, and landed in New York on the 8th day of July, thus making the sea voyage six weeks in duration. Mr. Adams settled in Mount Vernon in the year 1853. His wife Elizabeth died October 2, 1862. On the 20th of November, 1870, he married, for his second wife, Mrs. E. O. France, nee Wood, widow of the late Mr. Herman E. France, of this city. The present Mrs. Adams was born in the State of Vermont.

XXIII.

ELIZABETH BYERS.

Mrs. ELIZABETH BYERS, *nee* Oglesby, of the Third Ward, is a native of Pennsylvania. She was born on the 11th day of February, 1788, in Chester county. Removed to Crawford county, Pa., in 1820. In July, 1844, located in Newark, Ohio, and in 1854 took up her residence in Mt. Vernon. Mrs. Byers is the mother of seven children, four of whom are still living, two being residents of this city, Joseph M., and Miss Margaret, and two are citizens of California. The grand children number fifteen.

XXIV.

MARY BEACH.

Mrs. MARY BEACH, *nee* McNeal, of the Fourth Ward, was born in the town of Goshen, Litchfield county, Connecticut, on the 14th day of December, 1782. She married Mr. Martin Beach, of her native town, on the 11th day of October, 1802. Mr. and Mrs. Beach removed to Mount Vernon in September, 1832. There were born unto them ten children, seven of whom are still living. Mrs. E. H. Sprague is the only child living in Mount Vernon. A son, Mr. Levi Beach, and a daughter, Mrs. William H. Hawkins, are residents of Knox county. Mr. Martin Beach died in Mount Vernon, on the 23d day of April, 1859.

XXV.

LEVI BEACH.

Mr. LEVI BEACH, of Miller township, (son of Martin and Mary Beach,) was born in Goshen, Connecticut, on the 4th day of August, 1803. Mr. Beach married on the 8th day of July, 1824, Miss Martha Mills, of Mount Morris, Livingston county, New York, to which place his father's family had removed. Mr. Levi Beach and family came to Ohio in the year 1837, and settled in Knox county.

XXVI.

ABEL HART, Sr.

Mr. ABEL HART, Sr., of the First Ward, was born September 22, 1791, in Tiverton, Rhode Island. In May, 1817, he came to Ohio, walking from New York city to Pittsburgh: at Pittsburgh he took flat boat for Marietta, Ohio. In the spring of 1818 he commenced work at Cincinnati, and remained there until the following fall, when he came to Knox county. In 1819 he returned to Cincinnati and remained there until 1820, when he went to Parkersburgh, Virginia. After a stay of a few months in Parkersburgh, Mr. Hart went to Nantucket Island, Mass., where he was married, on the 29th of June, 1823 to Miss Mary Harris. Mr. Hart remained in Massachusetts until 1835, when he moved his family to Mount Vernon, Ohio, arriving on the last day of October, 1835.

In the spring of 1836, Mr. Hart built a house on the corner of Gambier and McArthur streets, where he has resided ever since.

Mr. H. was one of the Charter Members of the Knox Mutual Insurance Company, and was a Director of the same for twenty-one consecutive years from its organization.

Mr. H. became a Free Mason, June 24, 1820, at Parkersburgh. Joined the Methodist Episcopal Church in 1821.

Mrs. MARY HART was born on the Island of Nantucket, Mass., July 29, 1790. Died February 25th, 1864.

Unto Mr. and Mrs. Hart four children were born, all boys, still living—Isaac, William R., Marshall and Abel. Isaac is now a resident of Jasper county, Missouri, Marshall is a citizen of Ross county, Ohio, and William R., and Abel, Jr., reside in this city. Abel Hart, Jr., is a Lawyer by profession, and is the present representative of Knox county in the lower branch of the Ohio Legislature.

XXVII.

HENRY W. BALL.

Mr. HENRY W. BALL, late of the Second Ward, was born near the town of Bedford, Bedford county, Pennsylvania, on the 29th day of October, 1803. [Mr. Ball died on the 18th day of August, 1876, since this sketch was written.] Mr. Ball was twice married: both wives have passed from earth. Mr. Ball came to this city in June, 1834, and resided in his late residence, corner of Mulberry and west Gambier streets, thirty-six years, and was a regular voter in the Second Ward for the same length of time. Mr. Ball had born unto him nine children, seven of whom are still living. Four of them,—Frederick M., and Dallas, and Mrs. Dennis Corcoran, and Mrs. Samuel Chisholm, are citizens of Mount Vernon, and Mrs. William Harding, who resides near Gambier, this county.

19

XXVIII.
DR. TRUMAN WARD.

Dr. TRUMAN WARD, of the Third Ward, was born in the county of Rutland, in the State of Vermont, on the 19th day of July, 1805. His parents removed to and settled in Miller township, Knox county, Ohio, in the month of February, 1815, when the subject of this sketch was only ten years of age. This gives the Doctor, boy and man, at this date, a continuous residence of sixty-two years in Knox county. Dr. Ward removed to Mount Vernon in 1836. The Doctor chose for his help-meet and companion through life, Miss Eliza Maxfield, of this city, to whom he was married on the 1st day of November, 1827. To Dr. and Mrs. Ward nine children were born—six of whom are still with us in the flesh. Of the living, his daughters, Mrs. Sherman Pyle, Mrs. Dr. S. C. Thompson and Miss Victoria, and his sons Byron and Alonzo, are residents of this city, and Frank is a citizen of Mansfield. One of his sons, Jonas, died while serving his country during the late rebellion, as a private in the 96th Reg. O.V.I., while encamped about Vicksburg. Three sons of Dr. Ward were engaged in putting down the late rebellion.

XXIX.
MELVIN WING.

Mr. MELVIN WING, of the Third Ward, was born in the village of Queensbury, Glenn Falls county, State of New York, on the 8th day of July, 1804. Came to Ohio, November 2, 1816, with his father's family, and settled in Milford township, Knox county. In 1830 Mr. Wing took up his residence in Clinton township. In 1869 he removed to Mount Vernon, having purchased his present residence, corner Gay and High streets. On the 12th day of April, 1838, Mr. Wing married Miss Elizabeth H. Ash, of Clinton township, formerly of the State of Virginia. Mrs. Wing died in this city, on the 17th day of April, 1874. Of children, five were born unto them—four of whom are still living, viz: Edward, of Garrett City, Indiana, James and Maria, of this city, and William who resides on the home farm, on the Granville road.

XXX.
JOHN TRIMBLE.

Mr. JOHN TRIMBLE, of the Fifth Ward, is a native of Ohio, having been born on the 26th day of September, 1806, in Fairfield county. Fairfield county embraced, in 1806, the territory now known as the counties of Fairfield, Licking and Knox. During the year 1809, Mr. Trimble's parents removed to Knox county, and settled upon a farm in Morris township. In 1834, Mr. John Trimble removed to Mount Vernon, and in the spring of 1835, took up his residence in his present home on the Hill, on the west side of Mansfield Avenue. Of the county, Mr. Trimble has been a resident sixty-eight years, and of Mount

Vernon forty-three years, and has lived forty-two years in his present residence.

Mr. Trimble has been married three times. His first wife was Miss Nancy E. Drake, of this town. This marriage took place July 15, 1835. Mrs. Nancy Trimble died October 11, 1836. The second wife was Miss Eliza Day, of Morris township. This marriage was celebrated on the ——, day of ——————, 18—. Mrs. Eliza Trimble died on the 27th day of April, 1866. Again Mr. Trimble took to himself a help-meet, and on the 27th day of March, 1872, Miss Ruth H. Boyd, of Mount Vernon, became Mrs. Ruth H. Trimble. Six children were born unto Mr. Trimble, one by his first wife, and five by his second. The children are all living at this date.

XXXI.

JOSEPH S. MARTIN.

Mr. JOSEPH S. MARTIN, of the First Ward, was born in the town of Huntingdon, Pennsylvania, on the 25th day of November, 1803. Mr. Martin, with his parents, came to Mount Vernon in the month of April, 1811, when he was only eight years old. Mr. Martin has been married twice. His first wife was Miss Susan Thomas, of Delaware county, Ohio, to whom he was united on the 16th day of April, 1826. Mrs. Susan Martin died in this city in the month of August, 1852. In the month of December, 1854, Mr. Martin espoused, for his second wife, Mrs. Mary Barton, of Mount Gilead, Morrow county, Ohio. Mrs. Mary Martin died in 1869, near Mount Gilead, while on a visit to her brother. Mr. Martin is the father of eight children—four sons and four daughters,—borne to him by his first wife, all of whom are living with the exception of one son, James, who was killed at the battle of Gettysburgh, Pa., July, 1863. He was wounded on the 3d, and died the next day, July 4, 1863. Of the living children, Mrs. Elias Rutter, Mary and J. P. R., (Piney,) are residents of this city, and Caroline and Ella, are at present residing in Baltimore, Maryland, while one son, Charles D., is a resident of Lancaster, Ohio. Charles D. is a Lawyer of eminence, and, as a politician, has already made a reputation second to but few of the young men of our country. He represented the Lancaster district in the lower house of Congress for two years.

XXXII.
JAMES HUTCHINSON.

Mr. JAMES HUTCHINSON, of the First Ward, although only a few months past his 67th birth day, is one among the few old citizens of our city, and has been a resident for over fifty-six years. Mr. Hutchinson was born near Baltimore, Maryland, on the 16th day of August, 1809. His parents came to Mount Vernon in the month of October, 1820. On the 13th day of July, 1830, he married Miss Sarah Stahl, of this city.

In 1837, Mr. H. erected the large brick dwelling, (now owned and occupied by Mrs. Abbott,) near the corner of Gay and Front streets, and resided there for many years. In 1850 he built his present large and commodious brick residence, south east corner of Gay and Gambier streets, and in 1873, erected his store, a fine three story brick, on south Main street.

Mr. H. informs me, that in 1820, there were only seven brick houses in the town, and of those seven, three only now remain to mark the past. The building on the north east corner of Mulberry and Vine streets, now occupied by Matthias Kelly, Grocer, is one; another is the old Fifth Ward School House and Masonic Hall, on north Mulberry street; the third has been so improved and modernized that its past appearance is but scarcely recalled to mind even by but a comparatively few of the oldest residents, and to others its very existence is forgotten. At that time, what is now Mr. Joseph M. Byers' pleasant residence, north west corner of Gay and Vine streets, was but a small one story brick building, built upon the east end of the lot. That old building is yet there, and still it is not there, for the modern improvements have completely hidden it from view. At that time, this little brick was occupied by William Vore, a teamster. About the year 1825, Vore picked up and brought home a young lad named Lewis, whose father had been recently hung in Pittsburgh, for mail and other robberies, committed in the mountains. One day Mr. Vore returned home from hunting wild pigeons and other game. Thoughtlessly he left his gun standing in the chimney corner, without first examining to ascertain whether the load had been discharged. The Lewis lad picked up the gun and went into the yard to play soldier. While thus engaged, Joseph Glaze, the little son of a neighbor, who lived in a log house on the lot on east Vine street, now known as the Dr. Officer lot, came to Mr. Vore's for a bucket of water. Young Lewis, pointing the gun at Joseph, told him he was going to shoot him, pulled the trigger—the gun went off, lodging twenty-five shot in poor Joseph's breast. Joseph started for home, and when about half-way between Vore's and his father's house, fell dead in the road. His body was picked up by his sister Elizabeth, and carried into his father's house. Miss Elizabeth Glaze afterwards married, and became the mother of Anson Sprague, of this city.

Another incident of Mr. Hutchinson's boyish days, is ever fresh in his memory. In 1827 Mr. H. and his young companions were keeping Hallow-E'en in the usual fashion; (my readers all know what kind of a fashion that is.)   On the north west corner of Vine and Mulberry streets stood a hewed log house, occupied by the family of George Lowe, one of the inmates being James Lowe, a bachelor brother of George. James Hutchinson, although fully armed and equipped, had passed the Lowe house without firing a cabbage-stock, and had got nearly to High street, when he heard the discharge of a gun. On going back to Vine street, he found that James Lowe had fired a rifle at the boys, the ball hitting one of the legs of Ben Roberts just below the knee.   Ben was one of the boys engaged in the frolic. This occured Friday evening.   The poor boy was kindly treated by the physicians, and the wound dressed. On the Sunday following amputation was found necessary. In the afternoon this was-performed by Dr. Maxfield. But it stayed not the Destroyer—poor Ben died that night. From that day to this, Mr. H. says, he celebrated no more Hallow-E'ens. James Lowe, a few years afterwards, was killed by a runaway team while hauling stone for Peter Davis, south of the creek.

Of the limits of the town, in 1820, his present residence was the eastern boundary, West street the western, and the lot now owned by the Hon. Samuel Israel, the northern. East from the lot now owned by Dr. McKown, to that now owned by C. Peterman, Esq., and all south of Gambier street to the creek, was known as Shaw's addition, and was, at that time, a famous resort for the Indians to practice their games, such as shooting at a mark, running, jumping, and wrestling. Near where the pest house was built in 1875, Mr. H. says, in 1820, were to be seen the ruins of several Indian wigwams, and near by stood three large orchards of wild Plums, which orchards became, in the proper season, a favorite resort for the youth of both sexes, who had a penchant for the juice of the wild Plum, or to whisper sweet nothings to willing ears.

XXXIII.
MARTHA ELLIOTT.

Mrs. MARTHA ELLIOTT, of the Third Ward, relict of Mr. Samuel Elliott, was born in Philadelphia, Pennsylvania, September, 1799.   Moved to Mount Vernon in 1829. She has lived since 1831, (forty-five years) in her present residence on east High street, on the lot next east of the Court House. Mrs. Elliott is now in the 77th year of her age, and in the enjoyment of good health: in fact can do most any thing that a lady of forty can do, when strength and mind are required to work together. Mrs. Elliott, at the present writing, is visiting the Centennial Exposition at Philadelphia, and enjoying the society of the few remaining companions of her youth. Ten children were born unto Mr. and Mrs. Elliott, seven of whom are still living.

XXXIV.
BENJAMIN KERR.

Mr. BENJAMIN KERR, of Pleasant township, was born in what is now Licking county, Ohio, on the 14th day of April, 1800. He married Miss Rose Elliott, of this town. Seven children were born unto them.

XXXV—XXXVI.
ISAAC AND ESTHER GRANT.

Mr. ISAAC GRANT, of the Fifth Ward, is a native of New Hampshire. He was born in the town of Lyme, Grafton county, on the 6th day of July, 1795. On the 20th day of February, 1820, he removed to Orleans county, Vermont, where he resided until his emigration to the West. Mr. Grant and family came to Ohio, January 25, 1854, and took up their residence in Mount Vernon. He married Miss Esther Chamberlain, of Troy, Orleans county, Vermont, on the 10th day of February, 1822.

Mrs. ESTHER GRANT, *nee* Chamberlain, of the Fifth Ward, was born in Wethersfield, Vermont, on the 20th day of March, 1799. In the month of March, 1808, Miss Chamberlain, with her parents, removed to Troy, Orleans county, Vermont, and remained there until 1854, when she, in company with her husband and family, came to Ohio. While residing in Troy she was united in marriage to Mr. Isaac Grant, on the 10th day of February, 1822. Three children were born to Mr. and Mrs. G.: a son, Benjamin, and two daughters, Martha A., now Mrs. George M. Bryant, and Miss Sophia, all of whom are residents of this city.

XXXVII.
NANCY KINDRICK.

Mrs. NANCY KINDRICK, *nee* Morrison, of the Fourth Ward, was born in Pittsburgh, Pennsylvania, on the 18th day of October, 1796. On the 2d day of January, 1817, Miss Morrison married Mr. R. Kindrick, of Pittsburgh. In 1839, Mr. and Mrs. K., with their family, removed to Knox county, Ohio, and settled on a farm in Wayne township. During the year 1853, the family took up their residence in Mount Vernon. To Mr. and Mrs. K., five children were born, four of whom are still living—one, Gardiner, is a citizen of Illinois, while three, Reuben N., Miss Sarah and Mrs. Jane Norton, are citizens of Mount Vernon. Mr. Kindrick died in this city, in the 82d year of his age, honored and respected by all.

XXXVIII.
THOMAS KERR.

Mr. THOMAS KERR, of Clinton township, (brother of Benjamin Kerr,) was born in Fredericktown, Knox county, O., on the 24th day of September, 1803: (this was before the formation of the county.) He married Miss Martha Montgomery, of this county, but formerly of Fayette county,—Pennsylvania. Two children were the issue of this marriage,—a girl and a boy.

XXXIX.
DR. JOHN W. RUSSELL.

Dr. JOHN W. RUSSELL, of the First Ward, is one of the most eminent Physicians and Surgeons in the State, and has long enjoyed his wide spread reputation. The Doctor is a native of Connecticut—Canaan, Litchfield county, being the place of his birth, which occurred on the 28th day of January, 1804. The Doctor has been married twice. His first wife was Miss Eliza Beebe, of Litchfield, Connecticut, to whom he was married in the spring of 1828. Shortly after their marriage, Mr. and Mrs. R. came to Ohio, and stopped at Sandusky city: but in the fall of 1828 (November) came to Mount Vernon and cast their lot with our people. Five children were the issue of this marriage, only two of whom are now living—William B., and Mrs. Eliza Cooper, the esteemed wife of Col. William C. Cooper. For about twenty-eight years the Doctor and his family resided in the building where his office is now located, west side of Main, between the Public Square and Chestnut street, and for twenty years he has resided in his present residence on east Gambier street. Mrs. Eliza Russell died in the month of November, 1871, after a peaceful wedded life of more than forty-three years. For his second wife Dr. Russell married, July 31, 1872, Miss Ellen Brown, at that time a resident of San Francisco, California, but formerly a citizen of this city.

XL.
FREDERICK J. ZIMMERMAN.

Mr. FREDERICK J. ZIMMERMAN, of the First Ward, is a native of Maryland. He was born in Hagerstown, of that State, on the 24th of June, 1807. In the early fall of 1816, his father and family removed to Mount Vernon, and settled in a log house then situated where the residence of Mrs. John Irvine now stands, in the Second Ward. His father, Mr. Godlive Zimmerman, died in this city, February 22, 1845. For many years old Mr. Zimmerman kept tavern where Mr. T. B. Mead's Grocery Store now is. This old tavern building was removed, and Mr. Montgomery Brown erected a large brick edifice on the site of the old Zimmerman tavern. No doubt many of our old citizens rememter the "Zimmerman tavern." Like others of the old gentleman's nationality, Mr. Z. dearly loved his pipe or a good cigar. At that early day, tobacco was a luxury not easily obtained; but the old gentleman was equal to the emergency, as his son Frederick can avouch for, for many a horse-back trip has he taken to Lancaster, Ohio, an older settlement, to procure the weed his father loved so well. Judging from personal feelings, for a good cigar, or a pipe full of pleasant flavored tobacco, is one of my weaknesses, but few of the smokers of the present day, would take so great a trouble upon themselves.

Mr. Zimmerman informs me, that, at the time his father came here, (1816,) there was not a brick house in the village. The brick house on the corner of Vine and Mulberry streets, now owned and occupied by Mr. M. Kelly, was, at that time, in course of erection, the walls having reached the second floor.

Mr. F. J. Zimmerman was married July 7th, 1835, to Miss Sarah Colopy, of this city. Miss Colopy was born in Virginia. Her parents came to Ohio, and settled in Miller township, Knox county, and afterwards removed to Mount Vernon. Seven children were born unto Mr. and Mrs. Z.—six of whom are now living—two reside in this city, one in Akron, one in Jackson, Michigan, one in Chicago, and one in Mount Holly, this county.

Mr. Zimmerman was Post-Master of this city some five years, under the administrations of Pierce and Buchanan. Mr. Z. built the house he now resides in, on east Front street, and has dwelt therein for over thirty years.

XLI——XLII.

MARY AND CATHARINE PRATT.

The Misses PRATT, of the Fourth Ward, are both natives of Pennsylvania, who, with their father, William Pratt, came to Ohio, in May, 1819, and settled on what was then known as the Vore farm, one and a half mile west of Mount Vernon, where the family resided until 1863. William Pratt, the father, died in December, 1829. Mrs. Elizabeth Pratt, the mother, died in March, 1853. The two sisters, the subjects of this brief sketch, removed, in 1863, to Mount Vernon, as stated above, and now reside on west High street, a few doors west of the Baltimore and Ohio Railroad Depot.

Miss MARY PRATT was born at the Indian Manor Farm, Lancaster county, Pennsylvania, on the 17th day of January, 1797.

Miss CATHARINE PRATT was born in Franklin county, Pennsylvania, near the Maryland State Line, on the 10th day of March, 1807.

XLIII——XLIV.

MR. AND MRS. E. S. S. ROUSE.

Mr. E. S. S. ROUSE, of the Third Ward, was born of Revolutionary stock, in Pittstown, county of Rensselaer, New York, on the 23d day of February, 1795. Served in the war of 1812, in Captain Davis' Company, Colonel Carr's Regiment, General Eddy's Brigade, New York Militia. Came to Ohio in 1818; settled in Muskingum county in 1822; moved to Knox county in 1832, and to Mount Vernon in 1850. Residence for the last ten years, on east High street.

Mrs. P. M. ROUSE, wife of Mr. E. S. S. Rouse, is a native of Augusta, New York. Was born October 10th, 1798. Mr. and Mrs. R. were married March 1, 1820. They have raised a family of three sons and two daughters, all of whom are adults and married. This aged and venerable couple can now count their grand children and great-grand children by dozens, and may live to see the fourth generation of their descendants.

XLV.
ISAAC HADLEY.

Mr. Isaac Hadley, of the First Ward, is a New Yorker by birth. From the age of fifteen he has been a citizen of Mount Vernon, and has been honored by his fellow-citizens, not only with their confidence and respect, but he has been placed in offices of profit as well as of honor, and faithfully and honorably has he discharged the duties of his several posts.

Mr. Hadley was born in the town of Willsborough, Essex county, New York, January 14, 1795, within sight of the waters of Lake Champlain, since made famous by Com. McDonough's victory, September 11, 1814. In 1810, Mr. Hadley's father, with his family, came to Ohio, and settled in the county of Knox. His father, Mr. Smith Hadley, was born August 14, 1765, and died February 4th, 1850, aged 85 years, 5 months, and 20 days.

November 9, 1825, Mr. Isaac Hadley was married to Miss Sarah Davidson, of Mount Vernon. Miss Davidson was born in Knox county, on the 22d day of November, 1805, and deceased January 16, 1873, in the 69th year of her age. To Mr. and Mrs. Hadley were born seven children, six of whom are still living—four reside in this city, one in Iowa, and one in Bellaire, Ohio.

Mr. Hadley's public life has been a remarkable one, having, for twenty-four years, held commissions, either from the President of the United States, or from the Governor of Ohio. At one time, Mr. H. was acting as Sheriff and Post-Master, at the same time, for four years.

April 28, 1830, Mr. H. received the appointment of Deputy United States Marshal, and served as such for four years. During that time he took the census of Knox county, and in the discharge of that duty, he visited every house, and every family, at that time within the limits of Knox county.

August 12, 1831, Post-Master General Barry appointed Mr. Hadley Post-Master for this place, and he served in that capacity for about nine years. In 1832 he was appointed by General Bevans, Deputy Sheriff. In October, 1834, Mr. H. was elected and commissioned Sheriff of Knox county, and in October, 1836, he was re-elected, (without opposition,) thus, with his own four years, Mr. H. was acting as Sheriff for six years.

Mr. Hadley was appointed Clerk of the Court of Common Pleas, April 13, 1839, and served seven years, that being the Constitutional limit. In 1834, Governor Robert Lucas commissioned Mr. Hadley as Paymaster of the Volunteer Brigade of Knox county, with the rank of Major.

April 30, 1863, Mr. Hadley was appointed and commissioned by the President of the United States, Commissioner for the Thirteenth Ohio Congressional District, composed of the counties of Knox, Licking, Muskingum and Coshocton, and served as such until the close of the rebellion, and was honorably discharged.

Notwithstanding his four score years, few men in the prime of their manhood, can compete with Mr. Hadley in the discharge of the duties of every day life.

20

XLVI.
LEONORA DEBENHAM HARNWELL.

Mrs. LEONORA DEBENHAM HARNWELL, of the First Ward, *nee* Miss Debenham, was born August 16, 1799, at Rickinghall, Suffolk, England. On the 29th of May, 1834, she married Mr. Adam Harnwell, of Redgrave, Suffolk, England. In March, 1841, Mr. and Mrs. H. left England for America. In the fall of 1843 they settled in Knox county, and for thirty-three years have been numbered among our best citizens. Three children were born unto this worthy couple, two sons and one daughter, only one of whom is now living, Benjamin, who is one of the prominent merchants of Gambier. The recent death of Mr. Adam Harnwell, which took place at his late residence on Gambier Avenue, August 4, 1876, has left this venerable lady almost alone in this her hour of mourning and of sorrow. Mr. Harnwell was 70 years of age at the time of his decease.

XLVII.
JOHN POWER.

Mr. JOHN POWER, of the Fifth Ward, was born in Washington county, Pennsylvania, on the 17th day of November, 1805. Mr. Power came to Ohio in 1833, and settled in Wayne county: from Wayne county he removed to Coshocton county, and from Coshocton he came to Mount Vernon. September 26, 1833, he married Miss Matilda Settle, of Brown township, this county. Nine children were born unto Mr. and Mrs. P., eight of whom are still living, three girls and five boys. Of the boys, John B., Thomas N., James W., and Samuel, reside in this city, and George C. is a citizen of Wooster, Ohio, and is Clerk of the Court of Common Pleas of Wayne county. Of the girls, one, Miss Nancy, married a Mr. McCoy, and removed to Kansas, and two, Miss Melvilla C., and Miss Martha A., reside with their parents on east Burgess street. George and John are married.

XLVIII.
JAMES CAMERON.

Mr. JAMES CAMERON, of the Fifth Ward, is a native of Ireland, and was born in the county Derry, in the year 1801, the exact date and month we cannot ascertain. Mr. Cameron arrived in New York in 1851, and in 1852 came to Mount Vernon. In Ireland, Mr. C. was a farmer, while in America, the land of his adoption, he has followed Railroading, most of the time under Mr. William Henegan and his son John.

XLIX.
ARTHUR G. RUNYAN.

Mr. ARTHUR G. RUNYAN, of the Fifth Ward, was born in Fleming town, county seat of Huntington county, New Jersey, October 31, 1795. Came to Ohio in 1816. Mr. Runyan has been twice married, his first wife being a native of Geneva, Ontario county, New York.

L.

NORMAN N. HILL.

Mr. N. N. HILL, of the Fourth Ward, is, by birth, a native of the Green Mountain State, having been born in the village of Cornwall, Addison county, Vermont, on the 28th day of September, 1803. His father and family came to Ohio in 1809, and settled in Zanesville, where they remained some two years, and then, in 1811, came to Mount Vernon; the subject of this brief sketch being, at that time, in the eighth year of his age, where he has resided ever since, thus giving him a residence of sixty-five years in this village and city.

Mr. Hill married, on the 12th day of February, 1832, Miss Mary Shaw, daughter of Mr. John Shaw, of Mount Vernon. Three children were the issue of this marriage, only one of whom is now living—a son—John S., who resides on the Harkness road, in Clinton township.

In his early years Mr. Hill taught school, and afterwards became chief clerk in the mercantile establishment of old Mr. Samuel Mott, at that time one of the oldest Lawyers in the place. Mr. Hill has been an active and prominent business man all his life—a successful merchant—an extensive produce dealer—a large purchaser and shipper of live stock—a manufacturer of woolen goods, and now the successful manager of our City Gas Works. Mr. Hill built the large Woolen Mill at the foot of Main street, lately occupied by Graff & Carpenter, Produce Dealers, having also dug the race, and put in the water wheel. He carried on the manufacture of woolen goods, at the above place, for over eighteen months, successfully and profitably. Of late years Mr. Hill has devoted all his business energies to the management of the Mount Vernon Gas Light and Coke Company.

To few men now with us, does Mount Vernon owe more for its real prosperity, than it does to Mr. N. N. Hill.

PATRIOTIC SONS OF AMERICA,
LODGE NO. 31.

ORGANIZED, SEPTEMBER 23, 1876.

TIME OF MEETING –*Every Tuesday Evening.*—PLACE OF MEETING—Meets in Hall third story of Sperry's Block, Public Square.

First Officers:

L. G. Hunt,	Dist. Pres't.	Samuel Davis,	Commander.
S. C. Thompson,	Past "	D. W. Agnew,	Conductor.
W. A. Crouch,	President.	H. C. Parker,	Right Sup'r.
John H. Stevens,	Vice Pres't.	John Tousley,	Left "
T. H. Trimble,	Secretary.	John Y. Reeve,	I. G.
M. L. Mills,	Treasurer.	Henry Cooper,	O. G.

JOSEPH C. DEVIN.   HENRY L. CURTIS.

DEVIN & CURTIS,

ATTORNEYS-AT-LAW,

MOUNT VERNON, OHIO.

OFFICE—North-East Corner of Main and Chestnut streets.

D. C. Montgomery,

Attorney-At-Law,

MT. VERNON, OHIO.

OFFICE—Over Stauffer & Son's Clothing Store, North-West Corner of Main street and Public Square.

☞ Collections promptly attended to.

J. B. WEIGHT,

Attorney-At-Law,

MOUNT VERNON, OHIO.

☞ Collections throughout the State promptly attended to. ☜

OFFICE—In Banning's Hall, over Wolffe's Clothing Store, North-West Corner of Main and Vine streets. ☞Entrance on Vine street.

W. M. KOONS,

Attorney-At-Law,

MT. VERNON, OHIO.

OFFICE—In Israel's Building, over Knox County Savings Bank, north Main street.

☞ Particular attention paid to Collections in all parts of the State.

LI.
SARAH PATTERSON.

Mrs. SARAH PATTERSON, of the Fourth Ward, is now in the 73d year of her age, and is one of those active matrons, so few of whom remain with us. Reared at a period when both sexes were enured to toil and hardships, unknown to the present generation, she has preserved all her early habits, which enables her to bear the infirmities of old age with almost the characteristics of youth full of life and laudable ambition.

Mrs. Patterson was born in Virginia, in 1804. When only two years of age, her parents emigrated from Virginia, (this was in the year 1806,) and settled on a farm within two miles of Utica, Ohio, where she remained until a few years since, when she removed to this city, and took up her residence with her son, Mr. James Patterson. A part of this farm is in Licking county, and a part in Knox county. At that time a great many Indians made the forests of Ohio their home, and Licking and Knox counties, to this day, show many signs of their former presence.

Sixty-two years ago, when the subject of this sketch was only fourteen years of age, her father being from home, she was sent by her mother to a mill located near Mount Vernon,—(the nearest mill to their farm,) for corn-meal. Sarah performed the trip on horse-back, following the Indian trail through the forests, and returned home safely with the much needed article of food. At that time there was only one log-cabin between their farm and the Owl Creek settlement, and the settlement was mostly inhabited by Indians.

At one time, her father's family were all out of the house, at work on different parts of the farm. Imagine their surprise on returning to the house, to find their home in possession of six Indians, who had found the turnip patch, pulled up what they needed, entered the house with their plunder, scattered all over the floor the rinds, and were having a good time generally. Some were dancing, while others were turning the flax-reel, the humming of which afforded them great amusement.

On one occasion, an Indian Chief named Custo, came to their home, and requested them to make him a vest—which they did. The vest required three yards of Dimity. This will give the reader an idea of the size of this son of the forest. As payment, Custo gave the family a pair of scissors and a silk handkerchief.

LII.
JOHN LINN.

Mr. JOHN LINN, of the Fourth Ward, was born in Union county, Pennsylvania, in the year 1797, and emigrated to Ohio in 1844, and settled near Fredericktown, Knox county, and lived there until 1864, when he removed to Mount Vernon, and has resided here ever since. His home is with his son-in-law, Mr. James Patterson. Mr. Linn is enjoying remarkable good health for a man of his advanced age—now in his 80th year. At the time Mr. Linn came to Ohio, 1844, he says there was only one house on the flat between Cooper's machine shop and the old tan-yard at the foot of Lathrop's hill, as it was then called. At that time all the flat was one vast field of wheat.

LIII.
MARY BARRY.

Mrs. MARY BARRY, *nee* Harney, of the Third Ward, was born on the 10th day of May, 1806, in the county of Waterford, Ireland. Miss Harney was married to Mr. John Barry, of the county Tipperary, Ireland, on the 10th day of April, 1829.

Mr. and Mrs. Barry, with their family, left Ireland in the fall of 1849, and reached Mount Vernon, Ohio, in December of the same year, after a disastrous voyage of over fourteen weeks. A few days after sailing, when almost in mid-ocean, after passing a pleasant day in social chat over the prospects that awaited them in their new home, and dwelling sadly and sorrowfully on the deserted homes and friends remaining behind, and building many "castles in the air," our emigrants retired to their berths to sleep, perchance to dream, of the loved ones and of the absent. This vessel, like all others at that time, bound for the land of plenty, was crowded with hardy emigrants. To many that night "was the last of earth,"—many saw not the morrow's sun—that was to rise for them no more. Alas! when their slumbers were the sweetest, the awful cry of fire! aroused the sleepers, and awoke them to a struggle for life, at that moment the sweetest "boon to mortal given." The vessel was doomed! Every effort was made by the captain and crew to quiet the fears of the panic stricken passengers, in many instances, without effect. The strong minded and the healthy, in hours of safety, became almost imbecile and helpless, while the weak and sickly became suddenly endowed with a strength and presence of mind that showed their strength came from a source not human. Some, in their panic, to escape death by fire, sought it in the waves that laved the vessel's sides. Every boat was soon launched and loaded with precious freight—rafts were hastily made and soon crowded with the unfortunates, and then entrusted to the mercy of the winds and the waves. On the second day after leaving the burning vessel, the boats and rafts were all relieved of their precious loads. Then, and not till then, were many weary hearts made glad with joy, for their dearly loved ones were saved, but, alas! many wept, and would not be comforted, for their dear ones were not. Two children of Mr. and Mrs. Barry were numbered with those who perished.

Five, of the eight children, born to Mr. and Mrs. Barry, are still living. Mrs. Barry now resides with her daughter, Mrs. John Henegan, corner of High and McArthur streets, where she is surrounded with every comfort.

LIV.
JAMES WARNER MILLER.

Mr. JAMES WARNER MILLER, of the Third Ward, was born in Windham county, Vermont, near Battleboro', on the 8th day of July, 1807. In the fall of 1814, he removed with his father, mother, and three brothers, to what is now Miller township, Knox county, Ohio. His father settled in the woods. At that time only two families resided in the territory now within the boundary of the above named township.

The subject of this brief sketch encountered all the hardships consequent to the clearing up a new farm in a dense forest. At the age of twenty-two he left his father's farm, and entered a store in Mount Vernon as a clerk. On the 18th day of December, 1833, Mr. Miller was married to Miss Mary G., a daughter of the late Mr. Gilman Bryant, of this city. They have raised a family of ten children, all of whom are living.

As a farmer, as a clerk, as a merchant, Mr. Miller has stood pre-eminent as a careful, prudent, and successful man, and has, by his energy and fair dealing, accumulated enough of this world's goods, to render him independent, and to surround himself with all the comforts the decline of life may require.

Mr. Miller is a shrew business man, and knows how to secure customers, and, what is still better, knows how to keep them. If an article of merchandise, however small and valueless, and he has it not in his store, is called for twice, by different customers, he immediately orders a small lot, and his customers are supplied—they must wait—for no other establishment in the city could furnish the articles wanted.

Although nearly seventy years of age, time sits lightly on his shoulders, and to-day, he has all the appearance of a man in the prime of life.

LV.

JAMES MARTIN.

Mr. JAMES MARTIN, of Monroe township, is one of our forehanded farmers, and is well known by all our citizens. He is a native of Pennsylvania, having been born in Washington county, of that State, on the 7th day of February, 1807. He came to Mount Vernon, Ohio, June 18, 1818. At that time, Mr. M. states, there were no churches in the village, as it was only a small place. The first work he performed here, was raising potatoes on the piece of ground whereon the Methodist Church now stands, on north Mulberry street. Another piece of work he often alludes to, was his ploughing down of the old Court House, then standing on the north-east quarter of the Public Square.

Mr. Martin married, on the 12th day of April, 1832, Miss Sarah Rigg, formerly of Washington county, Pennsylvania. Miss Rigg came to Mount Vernon in the year 1830. To them were born two children, both of whom have deceased. Mr. Martin, his wife and six grand-children, now reside on his beautiful and fertile farm, on the Coshocton road, a short distance from the corporation line.

SILVER CORNET BAND,

OF

Mt. Vernon, Ohio.

WILLIAM M. THOMPSON, President,
S. C. SAPP, Leader,
GEORGE DAVIS, Secretary,
CARLOS H. WEEKS, Treasurer.

HOMER A. WEEKS,	SMITH GRAFF,
C. P. GREGORY,	J. MORGAN ROBERTS,
W. H. SPENCER,	ALFRED R. BELL.
JOHN MILLER,